To Tom x David-
all my very best
Wishes from
Shimon Peres

FANTASTIC!

The Extraordinary Life of

LINO PIRES

FANTASTIC!

The Extraordinary Life of

LINO PIRES

Foreword by David Hobbs

LiveWire
Books

First published in 2002 by
Live Wire Books
The Orchard, School Lane
Warmington, Banbury,
Oxon OX17 1DE

Tel: 01295 690624
Email: info@livewirebooks.com

Reprinted 2004
New edition 2009

ISBN 978-0-9553124-5-8

A catalogue record for this book is available from the British Library.

This new edition designed by Dick Malt

Printed and bound in Dubai by Oriental Press.

DEDICATION

For Augusta, without whose love and support
none of this would have been possible.

And for Peter, Helen, Heather, Edward and James,
who have made it all worthwhile.

CONTENTS

FOREWORD
by David Hobbs

When our family moved to Upper Boddington in 1966, The Butcher's Arms at Priors Hardwick, one of the few local pubs in the area, seemed to be suffering from something of a conviviality by-pass. Then, in 1973, Lino and Augusta arrived. What a difference!

Instantly the atmosphere changed as some of the discerning clientele on whom they had made such an impression during their time working at The Westgate Hotel in Warwick started to follow them over. At the same time, the first structural alterations were begun. Our whole family soon became regulars and at the end of that first year Dad decided that we should have our Christmas Eve family dinner there.

During the next thirty-two years, we missed just one Christmas Eve at The Butcher's Arms, a tradition that ended only when I and my wife Margaret moved to America in 2005. And it continues to be our very first port of call whenever we make one of our regular visits to the UK. As our plane touches down at Heathrow and we adjust our watches to local time the uppermost thought in our minds is always the same: "If we collect our bags quickly and get on the road sharpish we should be able to get back home just in time for lunch at The Butcher's."

What are the main factors behind the dramatic metamorphosis from sleepy little pub to one of the most popular and successful restaurants in the Midlands?

It is fashionable these days for retired CEO's and corporate giants to write memoirs in which they extol the virtues that made them and their companies successful. Leadership, hard work, personnel management, quality control, marketing, product presentation, good value and customer satisfaction are all duly cited. With Lino and Augusta, who arrived in this country from a tiny village in Portugal uneducated, inexperienced, unable to speak the language and with no assets at all, these attributes seemed to come as second nature.

A great team, they worked together tremendously hard but, as the Americans say, they also worked smart. While Augusta presided over the kitchen, Lino has always had an incredible financial grasp of what he can and cannot do and his son Peter, who joined the business full time in 1984, has clearly inherited the same instinct. They insist on the highest standards both from their dedicated and loyal group of helpers and from their suppliers and, in this respect, they lead by example.

Above all, the warmth of the welcome extended to everyone who comes through the door of The Butcher's Arms is irresistible. Over the years we have taken many American friends there and they are invariably bowled over by the experience. As far as they are concerned it has definitely got what is referred to in American corporate-speak as the 'Wow!' factor, something special that sets it apart.

In the early days, our great friends John and Helen Sadiq asked Lino rather apprehensively whether it would be OK for their then very young boys to eat with them. Lino instantly replied: "Of course. We need them. They are our future customers." How right he was. Between our two families, Margaret and I and the Sadiqs have five sons, all of whom have grown up spending a fortune at The Butcher's Arms. And now they are starting to take their own children there.

It is with great sadness and a deep sense of loss that I have to record that since I wrote my original foreword for the first edition of this book in 2002, Augusta has been taken from us. She died in the summer of 2008 after a brave, four-year battle with cancer.

For all her family and her many friends, but especially for Lino, this was a terrible blow. Married for more than fifty years, Lino and Augusta had a very strong sense of family – in fact, family was everything to them. They were overjoyed when Peter married Helen and the arrival of three lovely grandchildren completed their happiness. At the same time, they liked to think of their customers as an extension of their family and that feeling has always been reciprocated.

This was demonstrated in a most remarkable way when, back in 1998, one hundred members of that rather unique extended family of regular customers got together at The Butcher's Arms for a special fund-raising auction dinner in aid of the Royal Marsden Hospital, where Peter had just been successfully treated for cancer. This raised a total of well over £80,000 for the special cancer research fund set up by David Cunningham, the young professor at the Royal Marsden who had been in charge of Peter's case. At the end of the evening the professor told us in amazement: "We have charity dinners at the Guild Hall in London for five hundred people that don't raise anything like that much."

The success of that event and the outpouring of sympathy and support expressed in the thousands of letters and emails that flooded in following Augusta's death bear eloquent testimony to the very special relationship that exists between Lino, his family and the customers they have been serving so well for so many years and helps to explain why The Butcher's Arms is such a wonderfully unique establishment.

PAIÁGUA

By Heather Pires (2001)

Paiágua is where my nanny went to school
and it's where me and Phillipa play in the pool
Paiágua is inland away from the sea
Paiágua is home to my family tree

Paiágua in September has a Fiesta
and in the afternoons some people have a siesta
Paiágua at night mysterious but sweet
for my nanny to see her relatives is a real treat

In Paiágua everyone goes to the clubhouse
and to hear the crickets you must be quiet as a mouse
Paiágua is very derelict and old
but has an interesting story to be told

Paiágua is where my granddad's school mates
beat him up and made it hurt
Paiágua is where my nanny was born and grew up dancing
in the square with her Fiesta skirt

Paiágua church is where my nanny got married
in Paiágua they get their own water and they collect
vegetables that have to be carried
Paiágua now has a corner shop and a bar
and this afternoon in my granddad's village they're
opening a road made of tar

Paiágua is where my Pai was christened in agua and
where they play cards and pool
and where my nanny ran away from her teacher
with epilepsy at school

Paiágua has the biggest forest in Europe with figs, grapes and honey
collecting and selling these things is the way people earn money
Paiágua has lovely good dinner, breakfast and lunch
They have lovely grapes which I washed in a bunch

Paiágua is a lovely place; it gives me a big smiley face

PROLOGUE

It was two o'clock in the morning and only one customer was still lingering in the cocktail lounge of Warwick's Westgate Arms. Behind the bar, Lino Pires was tidying up after another busy Saturday night in what was then, back in 1972, one of the best and most fashionable restaurants outside London.

As Lino washed and polished the glasses and businessman Bill Kendrick finished his drink, the two men fell into a conversation during which Bill quizzed Lino casually about his long-term ambitions for the future. Lino proceeded to tell him, as he would tell anyone who cared to listen in those days, about his dream of one day having a place of his own and of the endless frustrations that he had suffered in his efforts to get started. "What I am really looking for, Mr Kendrick, is a nice little country pub."

Bill Kendrick smiled. "Really?" he said. "Well, as it happens, I have one that I would be very happy to sell to you."

The asking price was £30,000 and Lino, at the time, was earning just £17-a-week plus tips. Nevertheless, he paused only to establish that the property was freehold and that it was in Warwickshire before excitedly insisting on shaking hands on a deal there and then, sight unseen. "Mr Kendrick, the pub is mine," he announced, offering his hand. "Now tell me, where exactly is it?"

Today, The Westgate Arms is no more than a fading memory, replaced by a block of flats, while The Butcher's Arms at Priors Hardwick, the run-down little pub that Lino bought that night thirty years ago, has become firmly established as one of the foremost family-run restaurants in the country.

Its enormous success is a tribute to the drive, determination and sheer hard work of Lino and his late wife Augusta, the childhood sweetheart on whom he had a crush from the moment they sat next to each other at school in Paiágua, the remote village in Portugal where they both grew up.

From the humblest of beginnings in a poor peasant community, their rags-to-riches story is truly extraordinary. Or, as the irrepressible Lino himself might say, with a twinkle in his eye: "Fan-tastic!"

A POOR START

I was the first person in the entire history of my home village who ever learned to read and write.

Even the most elementary education was something of a luxury among the more remote peasant communities of pre-war Portugal – and you would be hard put to find anywhere further off the beaten track than Vinha. Hidden away in the backwoods of Castelo Branco, a country district some 200 miles North-East of Lisbon, this tiny hamlet was two or three miles from any proper road in those days and could be reached only on foot or by donkey. The nearest town, Castelo Branco itself, was a full day's walk away. With just nine houses and a total population of less than forty, Vinha truly was in the middle of nowhere. It was here that I was born, an only child, on May 21, 1933.

My future prospects at this point were not at all promising. You will often hear successful people proudly boasting about their rise from rags to riches but sometimes, listening to them talk about their lowly beginnings, I have to smile to myself. Compared to me, many of them sound as if they were actually born with silver spoons in their mouths. I really did start with nothing.

Even in the more prosperous villages of our mountainous and densely pine forested region of Portugal, people struggled to make ends meet – and Vinha was almost literally dirt poor. Like most of their neighbours and generations of my family before them, my parents, Manuel and Amelia, just about managed to scratch a bare subsistence living from their few acres of mostly stony, infertile land. They supplemented this with the little bit of cash they could earn as casual labourers on larger farms in the area.

My father also found occasional employment as the local slaughterman. Having once worked part-time in an abattoir, his services would be called upon whenever somebody in the village wanted to kill and butcher a goat or pig, either for some festive occasion or to be salted away in the large pine chests that were a feature of every household. For this he would mostly be paid in kind, perhaps with the hide of the animal or a little of the meat, usually the brains. Mixed with scrambled egg and fried, this provided a tasty alternative treat to the vegetable broth that was our staple diet.

Manuel and Amelia were simple, honest folk in the very best and truest sense. A devoted couple, and also very loving parents, they had no great ambition to improve their lot. They knew no other way of life than that into which they had been born and mere survival was their prime concern. At the same time, they were immensely proud people for whom the good name of the family was all-important.

My father, a quiet, gentle, unassuming man, was held in the highest regard not only in our own village but throughout the surrounding area. A measure of the respect he commanded was the fact that he would regularly be called upon to help supervise the traditional inheritance process whereby the head of any family, once his children had grown up and he himself was ready to 'retire', would formally pass on his estate to the next generation, splitting everything equally among his offspring. This would involve dividing up the property into parcels of land, each of which would be given a number, with the sons and daughters then drawing lots to see who got what.

Needless to say, such a delicate procedure had to be handled very carefully if disputes were to be avoided, especially in larger families where property might have to be shared out between half-a-dozen or more siblings in such a way that nobody was seen to do better than anyone else. Only the most honest and trustworthy people would be called in to serve as the independent 'referees' traditionally required to make sure that everything was done fair and square. My father was most people's automatic first choice.

Our own family estate was pathetically small, no more than a few scattered acres, much of it either pine forest or barren scrubland. We grew corn and vegetables on the more fertile plots down by the river and had a few fruit and olive trees scattered around on the rocky hillsides. There was a donkey to do all the heavy work, a pig to be fattened up for meat, a little herd of goats for milk and some scrawny chickens.

The ramshackle mud-and stone building in which we lived was little more than a shed. Clinging to the side of the narrow valley in which Vinha was located, it was shared not only with my grandparents, Jose and Maria, but also with my uncle and aunt, Luis and Alexandrina, and their two children, Diamantino and Adriano, both of whom were destined to work for me at The Butcher's Arms one day. Another uncle, also called Manuel, lived in an adjoining building.

Traditionally, newly wed couples would move in with the wife's family. As first my mother and then her sister got married, my grandparents had simply partitioned off another small section of the house with bits of hardboard, so that each family ended up with their own cramped, windowless quarters. My parents had their own tiny bedroom while I slept in the basement store room, my thin straw mattress thrown down in a corner next to sacks of animal feed and grain, jars of raw olive oil, strings of onions and the large wooden chest containing salted joints of pork.

There was no bathroom, of course, and the donkey's stable served as our 'indoor' toilet. Most of the time you would just go out and squat down behind the nearest wall or bush. We washed in cold water from a well that was a short walk down a muddy path, half-hidden under an ivy-covered overhang of rock. Fetching the water was one of my daily chores. Once a week we would heat some of it up over the fire for an all-over wash that was the nearest we ever got to a bath.

Our kitchen consisted of little more than an open fire in one corner of the main living area, with a sheet of metal that would be placed over the top of it to serve as a hotplate. There was also a pot for boiling the vegetable soup that was served up as the main meal every day of the week except Sunday, when we might sometimes be lucky enough to have a little meat. I still have that pot on display at The Butcher's Arms, a powerful reminder of my childhood.

I can truthfully say that I look back on those days without the slightest hint of nostalgia. The image of me as a young peasant boy, herding the family goats through the woods and across the hillsides (and later, as a teenager, using this as an opportunity to enjoy secret assignations with the pretty daughter of a neighbour who was doing the same job for her family!) may seem rather appealing from a comfortable distance, especially to anyone harbouring romantic illusions about the joys of a simple rustic existence, far from the stressful hurly-burly of modern 21st-century life. Sadly, however, the harsh reality of my family's daily grind was anything but romantic and from quite an early age I thought of very little else other than how to avoid following in their footsteps.

Portugal had one of the poorest and most backward peasant economies in Western Europe in those days and life in the outlying regions was extremely basic. With few roads, no electricity, no running water, no services of any kind and certainly no radio or newspapers, we were effectively cut off from the outside world. We lived mostly from hand to mouth, not only producing all our own food, wine and olive oil but also making our own bed linen and some of our own clothes from the flax that we grew ourselves and that the women would then spin and weave through the long winter evenings. We made our own candles and even our own soap, using animal fat and soda.

In some of the wealthier villages, the better-off families were able to make money by selling their surplus crops, mostly corn and olive oil. But in Vinha, where the land was particularly thin and poor, we were barely self-sufficient. There was never anything left over to sell. The only way of earning hard cash to buy those basic necessities of life that we couldn't produce ourselves, along with such little luxuries as sugar and coffee and occasional new clothing, was by working as part-time farm labourers for the handful of bigger landowners in the region. This would sometimes involve walking all day just to get there, then living rough on site. My father would often be away for weeks at a time, as would I myself when I was older.

Very occasionally, road building projects in the region would provide opportunities for jobs as navvies but, again, these would often mean setting out before sunrise on a two or three-hour walk to the site, wearing work boots roughly cobbled together out of bits of rubber from old car tyres.

Even as children, we never received birthday or Christmas presents of any kind and the only toys we ever had were home-made, tightly bundled rags sewn into an outer casing to serve as a makeshift ball, for instance. People also had to provide their own simple entertainment. In the evenings, the men would sit around playing cards and telling stories while the women would spin and weave.

Fishing was my favourite pastime, although the methods I employed would certainly be frowned upon by any self-respecting angler. I had no rod, line or tackle of any sort. Instead, I resorted to damming a section of the stream at either end before draining the resulting pool to leave trout and eels floundering in the mud. When I was a bit older, much to my mother's alarm, I would stun the fish with explosive charges made from gunpowder collected from fireworks.

The highpoints of the social calendar were the annual village fiestas, held in honour of the local patron saint. Vinha was too small to have its own fiesta, so we shared with neighbouring Paiágua, where the little chapel is dedicated to the Senhora Das Dores. This translates as 'the pain lady', very appropriate, I used to think, given the harshness of our everyday existence.

The fiestas were eagerly awaited. Musicians with accordions and guitars would provide the accompaniment for dancing in the village square, a goat would be roasted on the spit and there would be plentiful quantities of the rough local home-made wine. The girls would spend hours working on their fiesta outfits while the young men would wonder whether to blow whatever savings they might have scraped together on a new suit made up by the village tailor.

Friends and relatives would come from miles around to join the festivities and youngsters would think nothing of walking for three or four hours there and back to get to the better fiestas. At the same time, locals fortunate enough to have somehow acquired coveted jobs in Castelo Branco, Lisbon or Porto, would take full advantage of the opportunity to return in triumph and show off to the rest of us how well they were doing for themselves. We would note, enviously, how pale and plump they had grown – a sure sign of a good, indoor job and growing prosperity.

How fashions have changed! Instead of wanting to be thin and brown, everybody then wanted to be fat and white. That was what gave a man, in particular, real sex appeal. You could have any girl you wanted if you came back to the village looking sleek and well fed because this indicated that what you had to offer was a passport to a better way of life.

One grew up very quickly in that environment and by the time I was seven years old I had already made up my mind that, somehow or other, I was going to be one of those who managed to get away. I was also smart enough to realise that education was the key without which I could never hope to escape. This, however, presented an immediate problem.

The only school officially available to residents of Vinha was more that four miles away in Sarnadas, too far for an eight-year-old to walk each day. The school in Paiágua was a lot closer, less than two miles up the valley, but it was not officially open to anyone from our village because we happened to be just across the county boundary, in a different catchment area. This was why, until I came along, nobody in Vinha had ever bothered with the rudimentary state schooling that was available for children between the ages of eight and eleven, and why, as a result, nobody in the village could read or write.

For most parents, including my own, education was not high on the list of priorities. They were keener to have their children helping them out on the land as soon as possible. I, however, was determined not to miss out and, after thinking about it a good deal I came up with a plan that I then put to my mother. Suppose we were to go in person to see the teacher at Paiágua, I suggested, taking with us a little present of a dozen eggs and even, perhaps, a home-made cake. Might not the Professora then be persuaded to turn a blind eye to the regulations and take me in?

Being an only child I was perhaps indulged a little more than I might otherwise have been and after a lot of badgering my mother gave in and agreed to give it a try. And so it was, a few days later, that the two of us set out with our little basket of goodies and walked through the woods and over the hill to the single-room schoolhouse in Paiágua to plead my case with the teacher, Professora Cutilde Silva Cardoso.

With a population of around 250, Paiágua was one of the bigger and more prosperous villages in the area and the school was already overcrowded with more than forty pupils. The Professora, however, was impressed by my obvious enthusiasm, especially when my mother made it clear that the whole idea of our visit and our little offering had come not from her but from me. I played my part to perfection, turning on the charm and even managing a tear or two as I explained how much it meant to me to get a proper education. That clinched it and, to my great delight, it was agreed that I could start there the very next day.

Few youngsters can ever have trotted so willingly to school each morning, even though it involved a long walk there and back along a narrow path through what is still the largest natural pine forest anywhere in Europe. Here, in the silence, a sudden noise behind you in the undergrowth would make you jump out of your skin.

Wild boar lurked deep in the woods and there was talk even of wolves.

My route to school twice took me over the river that wound through the valley, crossing by means of a simple bridge formed by two tree trunks laid side-by-side. There was no handrail of any sort and in winter, when the stream was in flood and the water was gushing underneath, you would inch your way across, balancing precariously. Strangely, however, it was only when the water had been reduced to little more than a muddy trickle that I tended to fall in, becoming over-confident and careless and trying to take it on the run. I would then have to go all the way back home to clean up because I wouldn't have dared to show up in class covered in mud. Apart from that, my mother took great pride in my appearance and, despite the very basic conditions in which we lived, would always send me out well scrubbed and with my hair, even then, neatly combed and parted, much as it is today.

That hairstyle was a major cause of provocation in the running feud that I carried on with the village boys of Paiágua. They were always ganging up on me because I was an outsider and also, I have to admit, a bit too cocky for my own good. They soon realised that the one sure way to wind me up was to ruffle my hair. This would invariably lead to a scuffle in which, being heavily outnumbered, I would usually find myself on a hiding to nothing.

My only real ally on these occasions was a pretty little girl called Augusta Marques who would run to the home of an aunt of mine who happened to live in Paiágua, crying: "Come quickly, come quickly – they are beating Lino again!" whereupon my aunt would dash to the rescue.

I never learned my lesson. As soon as I got to the other side of the valley on my way home I would turn to shout insults back at my tormentors who, by then, would already be out tending their families' goats and wouldn't dare abandon them to give chase. The next day, of course, they would be waiting for me and the whole thing would start up again.

Augusta was only about seven years old at this time but, even so, her protective concern for me won my heart. Apart from that, she also happened to be by far the prettiest girl in the village! I therefore made sure, when she, too, started school, that I was sitting next to her. This was a further cause of friction with the local village lads, who all had their eyes on her.

Being a bit older, I finished at the school a year ahead of Augusta and on my last day I hid a little note in her desk, where I knew she would find it later. In it I declared undying love and asked her to be my girlfriend. It was all terribly innocent, of course. I was eleven years old at the time and could never have imagined in my wildest dreams what the future held in store for the two of us.

It was to be several years before we actually got together again and started formally 'courting'. In the meantime, my main concern was to organise an escape route out of the dead-end existence in Vinha with which I was still threatened. The rudimentary education I had managed to acquire was only the first step. To get any further I needed some kind of permanent job in town and for this my only hope was to find a relative or friend with personal contacts who might be able to pull some strings.

My Godfather, Jose Barata, was the one who eventually came up trumps, arranging for me to go and help with the washing up and other menial tasks in a little bar in Castelo Branco that was owned by a friend of his, Antonio do Ninho. After a year of this, I moved to a restaurant just off the town square owned by a wealthy Catholic priest, Jose Pardal.

My job here was to walk around from table to table, selling cigars, cigarettes and matches from a tray. It wasn't much, but I loved it. The work was interesting, I had a smart uniform that included my first proper pair of shoes and I was provided with accommodation 'below stairs' in the priest's large house. Also living there were some other members of his staff, including five young girls. This, as it turned out, was to be my downfall, temptation beyond endurance for any red-blooded young man.

After a couple of years, still aged only fourteen, I managed to get caught in bed with one of the girls and was sent home in disgrace. This was a major scandal at a time when, certainly in the villages, even courting couples were still very strictly chaperoned and a man couldn't so much as kiss a girl unless he was going to marry her. I had a terrible reputation for years afterwards and when I started going out with Augusta her friends and various members of her family tried to warn her off, saying: "You don't want him – he's too bloody frisky!"

To be honest, I was far more concerned at the time about the loss of the job that had been my hard-won passport out of Vinha. The priest was actually quite understanding, telling my father that he liked me very much and didn't want to lose me but felt that I definitely needed a bit more punishment down on the farm! "Work him hard and then send him back to me in six months' time," he said. He even agreed to carry on paying my wages in the meantime. I breathed a sigh of relief but then, before I had fully atoned for my sins, he died very suddenly of cancer.

I was right back to square one and this time there seemed to be no other easy way out. I tried everything I could think of but got absolutely nowhere, and as the months wore on I found myself gradually slipping deeper and deeper into exactly the sort of age-old peasant routine in Vinha that I had always been so desperate to avoid.

Our days would start well before dawn and we would then be out in the fields from sunrise to sunset. Every backbreaking job had to be slowly and painstakingly done by hand, from ploughing and sowing to hoeing and harvesting.

Corn would be manually stripped from the cob before being used to make the coarse-textured bread for which I still have a taste but which Augusta always detested. The traditional method of thrashing wheat was even more primitive. It involved finding a flat piece of ground over which to spread a mixture of cow dung and water that would then be left to bake rock hard in the sun. Rather surprisingly, this provides an ideal flat, hard surface on which, quite literally, to thrash the grain from the chaff with flails. Because the dung mixture never cracked in the way that clay does, there would be no crevices into which the grain could disappear. The grain would then be ground into flour on the village's communal mill, with six or more men required to turn the huge stone.

The use of cow dung in this process didn't seem to affect the aroma or flavour of the resulting bread in any way. We even used to joke that it must add a special aphrodisiac quality, which would perhaps explain why so many people in those communities seemed to have about ten children!

From October to Christmas the grape and olive harvests would provide welcome opportunities for seasonal work on the big estates around Castelo Branco. There was one place, in particular, where I would go every year to pick the olives. It would take me a whole day to walk there and I would then stay for up to three weeks, camping out in the barn with the rest of the casual workforce and living, at least partly, off rations that I had taken with me, including chorizo, beans and bread. There would be twenty or thirty of us altogether and in the evenings, after work, somebody would usually get out a guitar or accordion and we would all dance together, one of the more pleasant memories from this period of my life.

I also worked as a labourer with the road gangs from time to time. As it happened, my grandfather on my father's side had been killed many years previously in an accident that occurred while he was helping to build the road from Castelo Branco to the ancient university city of Coimbra. Working in a trench, he was buried alive under an avalanche sparked off by blasting operations nearby.

It was all too easy to imagine how this might have happened. At fifteen or sixteen years of age I myself was working with dynamite in circumstances that would horrify any modern Health & Safety Executive. Armed with a giant chisel and a sledgehammer, two of you together would drive a hole deep into the rock. There was a special knack to the way you had to hold and twist the chisel as your partner hit it with the sledgehammer, a knack I still have to this day. Once you had cut the hole to the required depth you would simply shove in the sticks of dynamite, light the fuses and run for cover, a bit like setting off fireworks!

At least this was more exciting than charcoal burning, one of my more regular sources of income. This involved going up onto some of the steepest and most inaccessible hillsides for a week at a time to collect the particular type of heather used in the process. The large root ball of the heather would be placed in a pit in the ground, set alight and then covered over with earth and left to smoulder slowly overnight to create the charcoal. The next morning we would dig it out, put it into bags and sell it to the local blacksmith for the equivalent of about 10p a bag. The great danger was that if it happened to rain heavily overnight while the underground fire was burning the whole lot would be ruined and you would end up with nothing for your efforts.

While all this was going on, I had once again re-established contact with Augusta, who coyly revealed that she had indeed found my little love note in her desk at school and had kept it ever since. In fact, she still had it until very recently when, sadly, it got lost as we were moving some of our belongings from one house to another.

I was seventeen and Augusta fifteen when I secretly started writing to her again, asking if I could be her boyfriend. It didn't remain a secret for long because her little sister Maria took great mischievous delight in spilling the beans to her father, much to Augusta's fury and embarrassment.

Hers was one of the better off families in Paiágua – her father was the local builder as well as owning quite a lot of land – and as mine was extremely poor I didn't appear on the face of it to be much of a catch. Her mother, in particular, didn't really approve of me at all, thinking that her daughter could do much better for herself. On top of that, there was the bad name I had got for myself as a result of the Castelo Branco incident. Her father, on the other hand, did quite like me because he could see that I was a worker and a fighter. He knew that with me she would never starve.

Although she was very close to her family and nervous about leaving home, Augusta nevertheless shared my dream of getting away, realising that there was no great future for her in Paiágua. For any woman, the traditional way of life in the villages was particularly hard. As well as having to look after their mostly large families, they were expected to do their full share of the backbreaking work in the fields while at the same time keeping their cramped homes meticulously neat and tidy and preparing nourishing meals out of a very limited range of ingredients.

Some of the imaginative cooking skills that Augusta learned at her mother's knee were to serve her well in the future, especially during the early days at The Butcher's Arms when she would produce endless meals for ravenous Young Farmers on a four-ring domestic cooker. Not so useful in Warwickshire were some of the other traditional arts she had to master as girl, including the ability to carry baskets and heavy earthenware pots full of water on her head. This was done using a special padded support frame to cushion and balance the load, some decorative examples of which you can see on display in the bar at The Butcher's Arms. Augusta could always remember times of drought in Paiágua when she would have to walk miles to fetch and carry water in this way.

She also became extremely adept at spinning, weaving and embroidering the beautiful linen tablecloths, napkins, place mats and bedspreads that she was to go on making for the rest of her life. At The Butcher's Arms she would spend much of her spare time working on a traditional-style loom that we had specially made for her by an old craftsman in Paiágua. Antonio Dias left Portugal for the first and only time in his life to come to Priors Hardwick to set it up for her.

As a girl, Augusta learned the lengthy and laborious process of producing linen from the raw flax that her family used to grow themselves. After being harvested in May, the seeds would be removed and the plants then left to soak in the river for a week. The flax would next be beaten with a wooden mallet and pulled through a piece of equipment known as a tasker to separate it, after which it would be smoothed and combed and then painstakingly spun into yarn literally by hand, twisted around the fingers. Finally, the thread would be coated in a mixture of ash and water to give it that special heavy linen texture.

Augusta used to have drawers full of the most exquisite examples of her linen ware upstairs at The Butcher's Arms, all of it decorated with intricate embroidery and lace crochet work. All those who have seen it have invariably been very impressed by the quality of her craftsmanship. A tablecloth of hers turned out to be one of the more sought-after items in the charity auction we organised recently in aid of the Royal Marsden hospital, fetching £1200.

Augusta was sweet sixteen when we officially started courting. You didn't talk about 'going out' with a girl in Portugal in those days. Being allowed *inside* the house was what was important, a sign that you had been accepted by her family and were enjoying a fairly serious relationship. I would go to see Augusta every Thursday and Sunday evening and these visits would follow a very strict, traditional ritual. After sitting with the rest of the family for a while, we would be allowed to retire to another room on our own, where we would sit on either side of the table and talk together while Augusta did her spinning. Any kind of contact was out of the question, not even holding hands was allowed.

Things went on like this for the next six years, during which time our main topic of conversation was always the same – namely, the need for me to find the sort of job that would enable us both to break out and find a brighter future for ourselves.

I looked everywhere, exploring all the usual avenues without the slightest success. It seemed that everybody in Portugal had got the same idea. If you went for a job you would be told that there was no chance, that there was already a waiting list of hundreds, sometimes thousands. I tried, in vain, to join the police force, a very popular option, but failed the exam. After being called up at the age of eighteen to do my eighteen months' National Service I even thought about signing on as a regular soldier only to find that there, too, the queue was impossibly long.

I would have emigrated, but that was barred under the dictatorial regime of President Salazar unless you had a definite job to go to, meaning that you found yourself in a Catch 22 situation. I had heard that there were ways of getting to Brazil illegally and there were even rumours about a Catholic father who was smuggling people out to France every week disguised as priests. I did think very seriously about that at one point.

Then, just as I was becoming more and more desperate, something happened that was to change my life dramatically, although not quite in the way that I had anticipated.

NO WAY OUT

Augusta always took great delight in telling people that we had to get married. It is true that I did suddenly find myself popping the question a little earlier than I had planned – but not for the usual reason. I had managed to get myself into trouble of a rather different kind.

It all had to do with a rather pretty girl from the nearby village of Almaceda. She had become the talk of the county, reports of her great beauty spreading like wildfire among the eligible young bachelors of the region. But it wasn't primarily her looks that interested me. Her most attractive feature as far as I was concerned was that she had family connections in Canada.

For anyone as desperate as I was to find a way out of Vinha, this was a considerable asset in any woman. As her official boyfriend one would have a chance of getting well in with her family and using their contacts to fix oneself up with a nice job in Canada. Not that I had the slightest intention of switching my true affections from Augusta, with whom I had been going steady by this time for nearly seven years. My idea was that I would just pretend to be interested in the girl and then string her along until everything was settled before finding some excuse to end the relationship as gently as possible. Augusta and I would then get married and go off to Canada together. Fantastic!

This plan, of course, had a number of obvious flaws. For a start, I couldn't really tell Augusta about it in advance because however keen she, too, might be to get away, she was unlikely to fall in with a scheme that relied for its success on me getting close to another woman, especially a very attractive one! At the same time, since everyone knew everybody else's business in those small communities and given also that Augusta had relatives living in Almaceda, there was no way she wasn't going to find out what was going on. Talk about courting disaster!

Not surprisingly, things all went horribly wrong from the moment word got back to Augusta that on the very day when I had been mysteriously absent from a village fiesta where she had expected to meet up with me, I had actually been spotted paying court to this other young lady in Almaceda.

All hell immediately broke loose. Augusta's family had always regarded me as a bit of a Casanova ever since the unfortunate Castelo Branco incident and as far as they were concerned this was the last straw, final proof of their worst fears about my flirtatious nature. Augusta herself was in tears and didn't want to speak to me, her sisters were wailing in sympathy, her brothers were out to get me and her father made it quite clear to her that I was no longer welcome in the house.

Urgent, decisive action was called for. My eye might have wandered once or twice over the years but Augusta was the only one I had ever truly loved almost from the moment I had first set eyes on her and I wasn't going to let her go now without a fight. I walked over to her house and begged to be allowed to see her so that I could at least have a chance to explain myself and try to patch things up. I got a fairly frosty reception but eventually managed to talk my way in for what was a tense and tearful confrontation.

I had to work hard to convince her that although I had been rather stupid I had never had any real intention of being unfaithful and that my interest in the girl from Almaceda had been motivated simply by the thought of what she might be able to do to help us both take a first step towards a better future. Augusta eventually accepted my version of events and although we certainly didn't kiss, we did make up.

Her family, meanwhile, remained understandably suspicious about just how honourable my intentions were. There was only one way to convince them. The following weekend, having first spoken to my parents to tell them what I had in mind, I went back and proposed. I explained that the only reason I had not asked her long before this was that I had wanted to get myself set up with a decent job in town first. I now accepted that the job would have to wait and that Augusta was more important.

The wedding took place in the little chapel of Senhora Das Dores in Paiágua in April 1957. Augusta looked fantastic in the white wedding dress that she had made herself with help from her older sister, a skilled dressmaker. I'm afraid I looked slightly less wonderful because I had managed to gash my foot quite badly while on another fishing expedition in the river the day before and had to wear slippers!

The celebrations were spread over two days, with plenty of feasting and drinking but, sadly, no music or dancing. This was out of respect for my grandfather, Jose, who had unfortunately passed away that same week. We had buried him in the little cemetery at Sarnadas da Simao, about an hour's walk from Vinha, where my parents were also to be laid to rest some twenty years later. The old man's death obviously put a bit of a damper on the proceedings but the wedding was, nevertheless, a happy occasion, with our two extended families gathered together.

Like all newly-weds in those innocent days when carefully chaperoned couples were hardly allowed to touch each other until they were married, Augusta and I had only one thing in mind as we waited impatiently for everybody to go home and leave us alone together! There was no honeymoon. Our wedding night was spent on a straw mattress on the floor in one corner of the room in which the reception took place, part of a building that Augusta's father normally used as a barn in which to keep some of his animals and their feed but which had been cleared out for the occasion. The next day we moved straight into my parents' house, where I had added a tiny one-room extension to our already overcrowded hovel.

Once all the excitement was over it was back to the old routine, with me now facing up even more urgently to the problem of how to find myself a decent job. For the first few months of our married life I was reduced to working mostly as a labourer for Augusta's uncle, collecting resin from his pine trees, a soul-destroying task that involved trudging up to ten miles a day from one stand of trees to the next on his scattered property.

What was particularly frustrating at this time was that although Augusta's two older brothers, Joseph and Francisco, both had top jobs at the five star Palacio de Seteais hotel in Sintra, near Lisbon, one as restaurant manager and the other as a wine waiter, they were reluctant to use their influence to get me in there too. Unusually, the two brothers had married two sisters, nieces of one of the partners who owned both the Seteais and the top-rated Tivoli Hotel in Lisbon, so it wouldn't have been too difficult for them to pull a few strings and fix me up with something. The truth was that it suited them far better to make sure I stayed put in Paiágua, helping their father to look after the family farm in their absence.

In the end, it was one of my sisters-in-law, Joseph's wife Esmerelda, who eventually stepped in and arranged for me to work in the Seteais where she herself was in charge of the bedrooms. I shall always be enormously grateful to her for sticking her neck out on my behalf. Here, at last, was the break I had been waiting for.

With the its mountain backdrop topped by the spectacular Pena Palace, built in the 19th century as a summer retreat for the Portuguese royal family, Sintra, in its heyday, was a favourite resort for the rich and famous. Now officially classified as a World Heritage Cultural Landscape, it was a place where European royalty and aristocracy mixed with the celebrities, tycoons and other top people from around the world who stopped off at Lisbon on the cruise ships. It was for this sort of high class clientele that the Seteais catered.

Grand houses and magnificent villas nestle amid the trees in the surrounding hills, discreetly hidden behind high stone walls and glimpsed through enormous wrought iron gateways while in the town itself the narrow cobbled streets and many historic buildings with their stuccoed walls in faded colours have an old-fashioned charm. In every sense, all this was a world away from anything I had ever experienced.

The job itself was very lowly – I was not much more than a male chambermaid – but the Seteais, itself a former palace, was already established as one of the plushest hotels in Europe. With a salary of 50,000 escudos-a-month (at a time when I was on just 750-a-month), its superstar French chef, Valier, was said to be the highest-paid person in Portugal, earning more than Salazar himself. And the regular VIP clientele included everyone from Princess Margaret to David Niven and from General Franco to Agatha Christie.

I particularly remember David Niven. He spent his honeymoon there following his marriage to Hjordis, and I actually got to serve him several times during his stay. My most vivid memory of him, however, involved Augusta's little nephew Joseph, who was also working at the hotel by then as a twelve-year-old bellboy. Joseph, who was destined to become our head waiter at The Butcher's Arms many years later, was too small to carry the heavier items of luggage and I will never forget the sight of David Niven hefting his own large suitcase while Joseph trotted along ahead of him carrying nothing but the room key. The Nivens, nevertheless, took to the little boy so much that when they finally checked out they made a point of giving him a huge tip.

Thirty years on, quite by chance, this most gentlemanly of all Hollywood stars came to eat at The Butcher's Arms but, much to my great regret, I completely failed to recognise him. He was in this country to make a coffee commercial for Banbury-based General Foods and was staying at the Hilton in Stratford-upon-Avon, very convenient for visits to the Royal Shakespeare Theatre. Having decided one evening that he would like to have dinner in a quiet country restaurant he went down to reception to ask for recommendations and the concierge kindly suggested The Butcher's Arms.

He was dropped off by taxi and the driver, who regularly brought people out to us, asked next time he arrived to pick someone up: 'So, what did you think of David Niven?' I, of course, had no idea what he was talking about at first and when he told me I still couldn't believe it. We had been packed that night and nobody had spotted him, none of the staff and none of the other diners. He had booked under a different name, of course, and had come in quietly without any fuss. Sadly, also, the ravages of the motor neurone disease that was slowly killing him by this time had already reduced him to a frail shadow of the suave, debonair figure we all remember so well.

I was terribly upset to have missed him, not least because I would have loved so much to have re-introduced him to Joseph and to have reminded him of the last time they had met all those years before. As it happened, the top executives at General Foods were all regular customers at the restaurant and when I told them later how disappointed I was that I had not been able to welcome him properly they promised that they would make sure he came in again next time he was over. But, of course, there was never to be a next time. His health deteriorated rapidly soon after that and it wasn't long before we heard the news of his death. It remains one of my great regrets that of all the well-known celebrities who have been to the restaurant over the years, the most famous of all came and went unnoticed.

All this was still a long way in the future as I settled into the routine at the Seteais in 1958, determined to make the most of the opportunity that had at last come my way. For the first six months I was in Sintra on my own, having left Augusta behind in Paiágua. The reason for this was that shortly after we got married I had bought a new house for my family. I suppose the ambition and the pride that has driven me all my life was showing itself even then. I was determined to move us out of that shed we had been living in all those years and when the best house in the village came on the market I went straight out and arranged to borrow the money.

I managed this by mortgaging our herd of goats in time-honoured fashion. The deal was that every time one of the goats had a kid, it would be sold and the proceeds split 50/50 with the lender. Even bearing in mind that the total sum needed to buy the house was fairly small, no more than about £30, it was still going to take a while to pay it off at that rate and once I had left home I didn't want my parents to be saddled with the debt. So, everything I earned during the first six months I was at the Seteais went towards paying back all that was owed and it was only then that I felt able to arrange for Augusta to come and join me.

I had managed to find her a cleaning job in another little bar called the Adega Das Caves, whose owner was happy to provide a room for the two of us just down the road, and that was where our married life really began. It was tough at first. For poor Augusta, away from home for the first time at the age of twenty-three, there was the sudden culture shock of being uprooted from the remote village environment where she never met anybody that she hadn't known all her life, only to be plonked down in a place where she knew virtually no-one at all

Naturally shy and a little unsure of herself, she found it all very frightening and felt, at times, a bit like a rabbit caught in headlights. She kept remembering back to her first ever visit to Castelo Branco at the age of fourteen, when she had marvelled at the existence of electric lights, something she had never seen up until then. The local kids had mocked her and her family as ignorant peasants and she suspected that people were now saying the same things about her in Sintra, gossiping behind her back.

On top of that, we were both working very hard. Augusta had to get up at 4.00 a.m every morning to start scrubbing the floors, washing up and cooking before then going off to market with the proprietor to help him carry back the shopping for the day. And although my official duties at the Seteais were confined to making up the bedrooms, I was always keen to volunteer for any other jobs that needed to be done, especially those that brought me into contact with the guests and gave me the opportunity to pick up new skills. I even went to the expense of buying my own uniform just so that I could work in the dining room in my spare time, learning how to serve teas and lay up the tables for dinner by helping out the regular staff and watching how it was all done. My wages were very small and the uniform cost quite a lot, but I knew it was an investment worth every penny. For me, that dining room was like a university of the world and I didn't mind paying to get into it.

At the same time, I was already keeping an eye out all the time for any opportunity to open a small business of my own. Ambitious as ever, it hadn't taken me too long to work out that if you really wanted to get ahead, you had to think about working for yourself, not for somebody else.

About six months after Augusta had joined me, what seemed like a golden opportunity presented itself. The tenancy of a little coffee shop in one of the narrow side streets off the main square in Sintra had become available. In an ideal location, with plenty of potential for development, it was exactly what I was looking for. The only slight hitch was that the owner wanted £100 for the lease. That was a considerable sum in those days and I certainly didn't have that kind of money. But I knew a man who did.

My brother-in-law, Francisco – the one married to Esmerelda's sister – had £100 saved up that was burning a hole in his pocket. So I went to him with a straightforward proposition. If he would invest the money in the coffee shop, I told him, we could put both Augusta and his wife to work there full-time while he and I helped out on our days off. As soon as we started making a profit, he could cream his £100 off the top. And once we had built the business up to the point where it could support all of us, he and I could quit our jobs and work there full-time ourselves. If we then found that the partnership wasn't working for any reason, we could start a second business on the back of the existing one, take one each and go our separate ways.

He initially seemed to think that this was a fantastic idea and was every bit as enthusiastic about it as I was. By the next morning, however, he had changed his mind completely. Having slept on it, he explained, he had decided that he didn't want to get involved after all. I was heartbroken. It was hugely frustrating for me at the time because I was convinced that we were on to a good thing and even now I look back with regret to what might have been. Although things have worked out very nicely for me in the end, I still believe that missing that early opportunity set me back about twenty years.

I know plenty of people who were setting up similar small businesses in Portugal at around that time and all of them are now multi-multi-millionaires. The country was ripe for development back in the late 1950s and although President Salazar's restrictive and isolationist regime was still holding back the economy in many ways, you could sense that a new entrepreneurial spirit was beginning to stir.

Further south, the Algarve was already starting to establish itself as a fashionable up-market holiday destination at that time thanks to Henry Cotton's early golf course development at Penina. And later, when visa and currency restrictions were relaxed and the package holiday boom really took off in the sixties and seventies, followed in the eighties and nineties by villa and timeshare developments, local businessmen who had got in on the ground floor were able to reap rich rewards.

In Sintra, especially, the growth of the tourist industry ensured that almost any business associated with it had a licence to print money. I have always been convinced that I could easily have been right up there with the best of them if only I could have persuaded my brother-in-law to come in with me to give us that early start. Instead, I found myself having to do things the hard way, moving abroad, leaving my friends and family behind, going through years of struggle and making many important personal sacrifices before I could get the foothold I needed to fulfil my ambitions.

It was on the re-bound from my bitter disappointment over the collapse of the coffee shop venture that I made the next of those vital snap decisions that have regularly changed the entire course of my life, almost always for the better I'm glad to say.

Staying at the Seteais in the summer of 1960 were a very wealthy couple from Leicestershire, Peter and Margaret Tahany. Mr Tahany ran a highly successful engineering business in Leicester and was a most impressive-looking man, a rugby Blue from Oxford who went on to become a referee at international level. He and his wife had two sons, Paul and Justin, and had asked the manager of the hotel if it would be possible find someone to act as a child minder for the younger of the two boys during their stay so that Mrs Tahany, pregnant with her third child, would have a better chance to relax.

The manager came to me and asked if I thought Augusta might be interested in doing the job. My first reaction was to say no, for the simple reason that she didn't speak a word of English. The manager, however, didn't think that this would matter because Justin was only three years old, which meant that there wouldn't be much need for conversation. All that was required was for her to take him down to the beach and generally keep an eye on him.

Having been persuaded to give it a try, Augusta proceeded to do such a good job and got on so well with the Tahanys that when the time came for them to return home they asked if she would consider going to work for them in England as a full-time nanny once the new baby arrived. The manager politely explained that this might be a little difficult as she had a husband whom she couldn't just leave behind. "You know Lino," he reminded them. "He works upstairs in the bedrooms".

They didn't see this as a problem at all, simply suggesting that as they also needed a gardener-cum-handyman, I could go and work for them as well. If it hadn't been for the fact that frustration over the collapse of the coffee shop venture was still so fresh in my mind, I probably would have thought twice about such a drastic upheaval. Although I had always been desperate to get away from the village, I hadn't really envisaged venturing much further afield than Lisbon or Porto and had only ever vaguely considered the idea of moving abroad as a last resort. But now that this offer was on the table I thought – why not?

I knew of many emigrants who had done very well for themselves abroad. We would certainly be earning more than we were getting in Portugal at the time so that even if things didn't work out, we could perhaps come back with enough money saved up to finance our own business. Augusta was very apprehensive, but my tendency in such situations has always been to go for it and she was quite happy to leave the big decisions to me.

Having said yes in principle, we still had the considerable problem of going through all lengthy formalities involved in getting passports and all the other documentation required to move abroad. In the normal way of things it could take up to three years to cut through all the red tape. As ever, the only way to get anything official done quickly was to find a good contact with enough influence to be able to pull some strings for you and here, once again, I was in luck.

Among the regular VIP guests at the Seteais was a very grand lady called Senhora Fernanda Bandiera de Lima. A member of one of the oldest and wealthiest families in Portugal, the Senhora's cousin just happened to be the Minister in charge of the Emigration Office at that time. For a lowly member of the staff to engage a guest in conversation was deemed a sackable offence but the Senhora was quite often in her room when I went to clean it and, in my usual way, I would chat away to her as I was making up the bed. I have never been afraid to beg a favour from anyone if I think it will get results so I took the opportunity to explain the situation and to ask very humbly if there was any way in which she might possibly be able to help me. She was most sympathetic and kindly agreed to write a letter right there and then that I could take with me to the Emigration Office.

Armed with this letter, plus the results of a thorough medical examination and a police report confirming that I had no criminal record and had never been involved in any illegal political activities, I duly presented myself at the Emigration Office to go through the rest of the formalities. Two days later, to everyone's amazement, I had my passport. People said that in getting such a speedy response I must have set a new record.

And so it was that less than one month after the idea of going to work for the Tahanys had first been mentioned, Augusta and I found ourselves boarding a ship in Lisbon, bound for England. All our worldly possessions were packed into a couple of cheap suitcases and we had no more than a few pounds in cash between us.

As the ship cast off, there were just a few friends on the quayside to wave us off. We were driven down to the harbour in style by Tony, the official chauffeur at the Seteais who is still doing the same job today, more than forty years later, and who remains a great friend. Our families couldn't afford to make the journey to Lisbon so we had said our goodbyes to them in Vinha and Paiágua. It was the last we would see or hear of them for four years.

Lingering up on deck to watch as our homeland faded into the distance and finally disappeared over the horizon, we had very mixed feelings about what we were leaving behind and the unknown future we were sailing into. Poor Augusta was already in floods of tears even before we were out of sight of land. For her, it had been difficult enough to cope with the move from Paiágua to Sintra. She had barely had time to adjust to that and now here she was setting of on a trip that seemed to her like the most terrifying leap into the dark. As far as she was concerned, we might as well have been going to the Moon.

Even I was a little bit anxious. I had no real idea about what we were going to find when we got to England or what our long-term prospects might be. At the same time, I was confident that we had made the right decision. I would have preferred to stay in Portugal but it seemed to me that our best chance of getting ahead there had come and gone. The Tahanys had offered us another opportunity. This time I was determined not to miss the boat.

THE GREAT ESCAPE

By the time our ship docked at Tilbury we were so excited that all anxieties were temporarily forgotten.

The Tahanys had sent a car to meet us and as we disembarked, clutching our suitcases, their chauffeur was waiting on the quayside, holding up a card with our names written on it in large capital letters. The whole three-hour drive to Leicester was then conducted in a rather awkward silence since neither of us could speak a word of English and the chauffeur certainly didn't know any Portuguese.

Augusta and I gazed out of the window in awe as the landscape unfolded. We had not known quite what to expect and our first impressions were of bright green countryside and rather dark, gloomy-looking buildings with lots of smoking chimney pots. It was 1960 and the Clean Air Act had yet to clear away the smogs that in those days still hung permanently over most industrial towns from autumn onwards through the winter.

The Tahany family home, Claybrooke Grange, was located out in the country, between the villages of Frolesworth and Claybrooke, about fifteen miles outside Leicester. From the moment we arrived, Mr and Mrs Tahany did everything possible to make us feel at home, despite the fact that any sort of communication was virtually impossible without resorting to mime and frequent references to a Portuguese/English dictionary.

This led to some comical early misunderstandings, our halting conversations being a bit like those between Basil Fawlty and his waiter Manuel in Fawlty Towers. On our very first day, Mrs Tahany, asked what we would like to do for supper. A Spanish omelette, perhaps? We nodded enthusiastically and Augusta duly knocked one up, which we ate it in the kitchen. Some time later

Mrs Tahany came in looking rather puzzled, and asked: "What about the omelette, then?"

"Oh, it was very good," we said with big smiles. "Thank you very much."

At this, Mrs Tahany burst out laughing and explained that she had actually meant Augusta to make the omelette for her and her husband, adding that she had deliberately chosen something simple so as to make it easier for Augusta on her first day.

Augusta and I decided we must take English lessons. We went first to the police station to see if anybody from Portugal was registered in the area but there was nobody. Eventually, we did manage to find a lady language teacher who agreed to give us some private lessons. At the same time, Mr Tahany gamely started trying to learn Portuguese, but on occasions this only led to further confusion. For instance, the Portuguese words for grandmother and bird are very similar – 'avo' for grandmother and 'ave' for bird. Augusta was therefore rather alarmed for a moment when Mr Tahany came home from the office one day and, choosing his words very carefully, announced that there was a dead 'avo' in the car. What he was actually trying to say was that he had found a dead bird stuck in the radiator grille.

Three weeks after we arrived, Mrs Tahany gave birth to her third son, Peter, and after that we settled into a regular routine. While Augusta helped Mrs Tahany to look after Paul, Justin and Peter and did some of the cooking, I worked in the garden and also helped out around the house.

Claybrooke Grange stood in its own ten-acre grounds and was very isolated, so apart from occasional bus trips into Leicester to look around the shops and to buy sweets at Woolworths, we were pretty much cut off from everyday life. Augusta, particularly, was very homesick so we went to great lengths to get hold of a short-wave radio capable of picking up transmissions from Portugal. Unfortunately, the signals from Lisbon were so weak that even with the special aerial that we rigged up we could never get any decent reception. We then discovered The Voice of Moscow, a Communist propaganda broadcast that was beamed to Portugal every evening at midnight and which featured a Portuguese exile promising a better life for everybody once the Reds took over. For some reason, this came through loud and clear and we would regularly tune in, not because we were closet revolutionaries but simply because we were so desperate for any kind of link with home.

Television was a novel experience for us, which we enjoyed even though we couldn't understand much of what was going on. Television had only come to Portugal in 1957 and very few people had sets by the time we left.

Even in England you could still get only black and white pictures, although a friend of the Tahanys who worked for GEC in Rugby had invented a sort of makeshift colour system. This was actually nothing more sophisticated than a specially tinted plastic cover that you put over the screen, but it worked surprisingly well. Our favourite show was the comedy series Bootsy and Snudge, which made us laugh despite the fact that we couldn't understand a word that was said. We didn't need to. Bootsy, the porter, had exactly the same uniform as I used to have when I was working in the Seteais and when he went through his trademark routine of coughing politely and holding out his hand behind his back for a tip we would be in fits.

We had been with the Tahanys for two years when the language difficulties caused a rather unexpected problem. Little Peter was still not talking properly and when his worried parents took him to see a specialist to find out why, it was suggested that he might be confused because of the way Augusta and I were speaking Portuguese around him most of the time. It obviously didn't cause any long-term problems because Peter, after whom we later named our own son and who is still a close friend, went on to become a high-powered and extremely successful lawyer in London and also, as it happens, owns restaurants. However, it was decided at the time that it might help if he had an English nanny.

Obviously, in this situation, Augusta and I were no longer needed but Mr Tahany, as always, was more than fair. Unless we preferred to go back to Portugal, he explained, he would use his influence to find us new jobs in England.

Augusta and I had a think about it and agreed between ourselves that although we were missing our families terribly, we weren't quite ready to go back to Portugal. When we had left to come to England I had promised myself that I would not return until I could do so in style. Pride demanded that I had to be able to go back with my head held high, to show that I had made it, to flaunt my success a little. In that respect there was still quite a long way to go.

Apart from that, we had already grown to like England and everything it had to offer. So we chose to stay and Mr Tahany duly fixed us up with jobs at The Three Horse Shoes hotel in Rugby – Augusta as a chambermaid and myself as a waiter in the restaurant.

Run by Jack Spencer, formerly restaurant manager at the Savoy Grill, The Three Horse Shoes had the reputation of being the best hotel restaurant anywhere outside London at the time. If that seems surprising, you have to remember that eating out in those days was not nearly as commonplace as it is now and really top restaurants were few and far between in the provinces. At the same time, the Midlands, particularly the area around Coventry, had become increasingly affluent in the post-war years, thanks largely to the boom in the motor and engineering industries, and as a result there was a growing demand for five-star establishments to match what was on offer in the West End, not just in terms of the food itself but also, more importantly, in the style of presentation and service. Recognising this trend, the owners of The Three Horse Shoes, which was ideally situated in the very heart of the region's executive belt, brought Jack Spencer up from the Savoy, along with a couple of the chefs there.

A former army sergeant who had grown up in the East End of London, Jack ran the restaurant with old-fashioned, military-style discipline. That suited me fine because I have always been a great believer in discipline and I don't mind having to follow strict rules. At least, then, you know exactly where you stand. I had actually rather enjoyed my time in the Army as a National Serviceman in Portugal for that very reason. With Jack Spencer everything had to be just so and if you made the slightest mistake he was onto it in a flash. Once again, this was no problem for me because I had already been taught the same impeccably high standards at the Seteais.

Apart from that, I was happy to put everything I had into the job because I was so keen to get on and I soon realised I could learn a lot from this man.

Nothing was ever too much trouble as far as I was concerned. I went out of my way to be friendly and obliging and as a result the customers soon started to notice me and to like me very much, as did the boss. The only people who weren't so happy about this were the Italians who made up the majority of the waiting staff.

The Italians make terrific waiters, absolutely brilliant. It's all in the fingers, something to do with the deft way in which they handle the cutlery. They are, without doubt, the best in the world and if I tried for the rest of my life I don't think I could ever be as good as they are.

The Italians at the Three Horse Shoes, who had come up from London with Jack Spencer, were especially slick. As workmates, however, they were not all quite so wonderful as far as I was concerned. Jealous of all the praise I was getting, they made up their minds to take me down a peg or two and started a dirty tricks campaign deliberately aimed at getting me into trouble.

They knew, for instance, that Jack Spencer subscribed rigidly to the view that if a customer ever had to ask for anything – salt, pepper, an item of cutlery or an ashtray – it was as bad as a complaint, evidence that you had not been doing your job properly in the first place. So, for instance, when I was serving coffee, one of the other waiters would come along behind my back when I wasn't looking and surreptitiously remove the sugar from the table. As soon as Jack then heard the customer calling for sugar, he would go mad, racing into the kitchen to find out who was responsible. "Who served the coffee on table six?" he would roar. "You, Lino? So, why didn't you bring the sugar?" My insistence that I had not forgotten it would be to no avail and I would be given a severe dressing down.

This sort of thing happened several times until one day Mrs Spencer, who always used to dine in the restaurant, spotted exactly what the others were up to. She later told her husband and suggested that, to avoid an awkward situation, he should think about taking me out of the restaurant and putting me in the bar instead. "I think Lino will do very well in the bar," she said.

Fortunately, Jack listened to her advice and duly installed me in the bar, where I was effectively my own boss. Even now I get excited when I think back and remember how thrilled I was to get that promotion. What I didn't know until much later was that spies had been put to work on the other side of the bar to check up on me. Mr and Mrs Bishop, a lovely couple who used to run K Shoes in Rugby and who afterwards became great friends of mine, were asked, as regular customers, to keep an eye out just to make absolutely sure that I was honest and that I wasn't working any of the traditional barman's fiddles. Once they had reported favourably, I never looked back.

I became a real star in that bar. Charming everybody with my fractured English, I made a point of remembering every customer by name and took careful note of their drinking habits so that I always had their favourite tipple ready before they had even asked for it. For the very first time in my working life I was absolutely in my element. Suddenly the place was packed every night and people were making a point of going up to the boss and telling him: "What a lovely move, Mr Spencer. Fantastic! Now you've got the perfect man in the bar."

My wages had risen to £12-a-week plus tips, which was not at all bad by the standards of that time. And with Augusta also working and everything going so well, we felt able to move out of the succession of rather dingy rented rooms we had been living in up until then and into a home of our own. We paid £2000 for a little place in Lowford Road, Rugby, bought with the help of an interest-free loan from Bill Wallace, one of the directors of the company that owned The Three Horse Shoes. At the same time we also decided that we could at last afford to start a family.

There was an early disappointment when Augusta suffered a miscarriage. Too much running up and down stairs in her job as a chambermaid, said the doctor. So, when she became pregnant again, she immediately gave up work altogether, even though this put us under a bit of pressure financially.

Peter was born at St Mary's Hospital, Rugby on February 4th, 1964. But with international communications nothing like they are today, the news of his arrival didn't reach our families in Portugal until almost a week later. There were still no telephones anywhere near Paiágua and the letter and photographs that I sent off would have gone no further, officially, than the county post office in Castelo Branco. There the package would have remained until somebody from our area happened to come in, whereupon they would have been asked to drop it off at the café in Sarnadas, the nearest local collection point to Vinha and Paiágua. Either my parents or somebody from Augusta's family would have then picked it up from there when they walked over to the church in Sarnadas for mass on Sunday.

A few months later, as soon as Peter was old enough to fly, we made plans for our first holiday visit back to Portugal since leaving four years before. I felt I had now satisfied the main requirements necessary for a triumphant return. I was doing well, I had a son and I had also acquired that other very important status symbol – my first car

The second-hand turquoise Ford Capri, for which I had paid what was then the princely sum of £450, would ensure that I not only got a hero's welcome from family and friends in Vinha and Paiágua but also that I would be the envy of former colleagues at the Seteais in Sintra. I wanted to show off as much as possible and, to put the icing on the cake, I set up an arrangement that I knew would enable me to make a suitably grand entrance.

I had persuaded my two bosses at The Three Horse Shoes, Jack Spencer and Bill Wallace, to take a holiday at the Seteais immediately before I went over. Then, having organised to ship my car out in advance, I offered them the use of it during their stay. Only four members of the staff at the Seteais at that time owned cars, including the Managing Director, Augusta's two brothers and the Head Porter, so I knew that this would cause a stir. Everywhere Jack and Bill went people would be whispering to each other, saying: "Look, that's Lino's car –and those are his bosses driving around in it! Lino must be doing really well!" Sure enough, the gossip soon spread all around Sintra so that by the time I arrived there to pick up the car, everybody was already talking about me.

I was a very proud man. Our homecoming to Vinha and Paiágua that first time was a hugely emotional experience. In the four years that we had been away we had been in touch with our families only by letter and as my parents couldn't read or write they had had to find somebody from one of the neighbouring villages to tell them what I had written.

Nothing much had changed in our absence except that one of my cousins, who had been working in Angola as a JCB driver with Augusta's brother-in-law, Francisco, had come home, hired a digger and taken it upon himself to cut a makeshift road from Paiágua to Vinha. This meant that I was able to drive the Capri right up to my parents' house, arriving with an extra flourish.

Everyone was ooh-ing and ah-ing over Peter, who was christened while we were there in the little church where Augusta and I had been married, and for the next month we were the centre of attention. There were endless parties and family re-unions and we had to keep telling our story over and over again. People wanted to know everything there was to know about England and every detail about our lives there. They never seemed to tire of listening to our descriptions of what the people were like, what we thought of the towns, the cities, the cars, the weather and anything else we cared to talk about.

For some of them, including my parents, it was all totally bewildering. In 1964, the older generation in the villages still had very little idea about what was going on in the world beyond Castelo Branco. Some had lived their entire lives without ever venturing further than walking distance from the village. Until I brought a transistor radio with me from England as a present for my parents on that first visit, nobody in Vinha had ever had a radio in their house.

We stayed for a month, dividing our time between the two family homes and getting used, once again, to living without many of the mod cons to which we had become accustomed in England but revelling in our local celebrity status. Before we eventually left to come back to England, I was able to confirm my new standing in the community in a way that gave me particular satisfaction.

Augusta's father had decided that the time had come to hand on the family estate to his six children and so the whole clan gathered together in his house for the formal sharing out of the property. Also present were my parents. As soon as the traditional drawing of lots had been completed, one of Augusta's brothers-in-law made it clear that he and his wife planned to sell their portion straightaway and so, in front of everybody, I stood up there and then and offered to buy it from him. He named a price and I agreed it on the spot.

I didn't particularly want the land – I later sold it and put the money towards a first holiday home in Sintra, not far from where the present villa is located – but I simply wanted to make the point that I was now a man of substance, that I had risen to become the equal of anyone in Augusta's family. In front of her parents and my parents, it again gave me great pride to be able to make such a gesture. The moment was made all the sweeter by the fact that the brother-in-law whose share I had bought had always looked down on me, maintaining that Augusta would have done much better to have married his brother.

When our month was finally up, we said our goodbyes, piled into the Capri and drove all the way back to Rugby. The 1,500-mile journey took only two days, without the need for any night driving, an indication of how little traffic there was on the roads in those days. Some eighteen years later Peter was to make the same trip in less than twenty-four hours, non-stop, but, of course, he has never been quite such a steady driver as his father!

Back at The Three Horse Shoes, things continued to go well until a few months after our return when Jack Spencer suddenly announced that he was leaving to set up on his own. Along with his brother Fred, who had been working for the same group in The Bowler Hat Club in Birkenhead, he had bought a pub called The Old Bowling Green, just off the market square in Warwick. This they planned to refurbish completely and re-open as The Westgate Arms, catering for the same up-market clientele as The Three Horse Shoes.

Despite the fact that they were going to be setting up in direct competition, they had managed to get financial backing from the owners of The Three Horse shoes – on the one condition that they didn't try to take me with them. It was a flattering measure of the reputation I had built for myself as a barman that they were afraid their customers would immediately follow me.

Unfortunately, things were never the same at The Three Horse Shoes once Jack Spencer had gone. The man brought in to replace him wasn't in the same league. There was no longer the same discipline either in the restaurant or the kitchen, with everybody allowed to do pretty much what they wanted, and the result was that the high standards of service and presentation soon started to fall. I watched in disgust as the whole business began to fall apart in front of my very eyes. At the same time, almost overnight, The Westgate Arms became established as the outstanding restaurant in the area. Within a week of opening it was fully booked every night.

I remained at The Three Horse Shoes for a year after Jack Spencer had gone but as the situation there steadily declined I became increasingly unhappy. People were queuing up to offer me good jobs elsewhere but The Westgate was the only place I really wanted to be. The problem was that the Spencers were contractually bound not to employ me there for at least three years.

In the end, I decided that desperate measures were called for. Believing, as I've always done, that you should go right to the top if you want results, I made an appointment to meet Cyril Porter, the Chairman of the group that owned The Three Horse Shoes, arranging to meet him at his home near Oxford to discuss my situation.

I then told him bluntly: "Look, what you have done for me is fantastic and I appreciate it very much. But I can't get on with the new manager and I am going to give in my notice and leave.

"The deal you have got with the Spencers means that I can't go to the Westgate now, but you know that I *will* go there eventually. And in the meantime I am likely to end up working for someone else in the same area. If you value me so highly, it surely makes more sense to let me move to an establishment in which you have a vested interest rather than forcing me to go elsewhere, possibly to a rival. You will gain nothing by that."

I had a strong hand and I knew that a good businessman would see the sense of what I was suggesting. After hearing me out, Mr Porter said nothing but simply picked up the phone, called the manager at The Three Horse Shoes and told him: "Lino wants to start working at The Westgate next month and I've agreed to let him go. You'd better start looking for his replacement right away."

This was 1966 and the most exciting decade since the Roaring Twenties was in full swing. From the outside, The Westgate Arms may have been nothing much to look at, but the five-star quality created inside by the Spencers soon turned the place into a magnet for everyone who was anyone in the Midlands. Captains of industry, self-made tycoons and leading figures from both the county set and the local business and professional communities were soon rubbing shoulders with top politicians, media personalities and occasional stars from the worlds of sport and show business.

It was a rich, powerful mix that I found irresistible. Not that I had much direct contact with them during my first stint at The Westgate. Jack Spencer started me off in the Town Bar, a public bar that was quite separate from the restaurant. This had proved to be a bit of a white elephant, not used that much, and my job was to build up the business there. This I duly did, very quickly filling the place up every evening of the week.

Without the glamour and excitement of the cocktail bar – and, more to the point, without any of the big tips – it was also very, very hard work. We didn't, for instance, have the luxury of automatic dishwashers at that time and at the end of the evening every glass in the entire establishment would come back to me to be washed by hand. As a result, it would often be two o'clock in the morning before I was finished for the night. My arms used to ache the whole time and I would walk home to the little flat we were renting just down the road in St John's Court and complain to Augusta: "I must be the highest-paid washer-up in the country!"

Meanwhile, I had never lost sight of my long-term ambition, which had always been to have my own business, and this now became my No 1 priority. Getting started, however, was not easy. A little freehold pub was what I dreamed about, but at that time there were very few free houses around, probably no more than half-a-dozen in the whole of Warwickshire. The breweries controlled everything.

After a lot of fruitless searching, it became obvious that I would have to settle for a tenancy to begin with and so I proceeded to write off to twenty-five different breweries. The fact that I had only a few hundred pounds to put towards the tenancy ruled out the sort of picturesque country pub that, ideally, I would have liked. What I was eventually offered, in early 1968, was the Railway Inn in Leicester.

Augusta and I went to have a look at it with four-year-old Peter in tow. Located in a rather grimy, unattractive downtown area, with the railway station on one side and the GPO headquarters on the other, this run-down alehouse was hardly the stuff of our dreams. And the regulars were certainly not the sort of high-class clientele we had been used to at The Three Horse Shoes and The Westgate.

Augusta was horrified. She was already anxious about me giving up the security of my job at The Westgate and unhappy about the prospect of having to move out of our comfortable little flat in Warwick, so she had been reluctant even to consider a move to Leicester. We were still rowing about it as we prepared to drive over and I was in such a state that I made a mess of backing out of the garage and dented the wing of my car, a prized Volvo 122S.

When, at last, we got there, Augusta's worst fears were soon confirmed. The place was filthy and looked as if it hadn't been touched for twenty or thirty years. As we were shown around the gloomy Victorian building, we counted no less than fifty-two doors, all of which clearly needed scrubbing down. Poor Augusta. The more she saw, the further her face fell and I could tell she was close to tears. But I wasn't to be put off.

I told her: "Trust me. We have to look forward to the long-term future and the only way for us to go up is first to go down for a while. Beggars can't be choosers, but if we work hard and make a go of this place we will soon be able to move on to something better."

Having barely managed to convince her that it was the right move, I went straight back and gave my notice in at The Westgate Arms. Jack Spencer was not at all happy about it, although he understood exactly why I was going. He had, after all, taken the same sort of chance when he left the Savoy. "Good luck, Lino," he said tersely when I finally took my leave, adding with a thin smile: "At least I don't have to worry about you taking any of our customers with you where you're going!"

A WAITING GAME

We had to wait several weeks before catching our first glimpse of a female customer at The Railway Inn.

Very much a working man's pub, it catered almost exclusively for male employees from the post office and the railway station nearby who would flood into the place during their lunch hours, at the end of their shifts and during their 'tea' breaks. For long periods of the day the place would be empty, then suddenly the bar would be briefly invaded by thirsty workers on a short, 15-minute break, all fighting their way to the bar simultaneously and demanding to get served as quickly as possible in the hope of getting at least a couple of rounds in before they had to shoot back to work.

They drank only beer, mostly mild rather than bitter in those days, and would be knocking back the pints almost faster than we could pull them. Inevitably, in this situation, there would often be angry, impatient accusations of queue jumping, with the added complication that some of the more mischievous black customers were quite adept at playing the racism card, insisting that they had been there long before the whites you happened to have served ahead of them and claiming that they had only been ignored because of their colour. If you gave in to them, the white customers would then accuse you of reverse discrimination. It was definitely a no-win situation.

Augusta and I immediately set about trying to raise the tone. We cleaned the whole place up, persuaded the brewery to put in some better furniture and started serving a small selection of good simple home-made bar snacks such as ham salads, gammon and egg and chicken casserole. At the same time, I went out of my way to be as friendly and welcoming as possible towards the customers, one or two of whom eventually responded by bringing their wives and girlfriends along for a meal in the evenings and at weekends. Saturday and Sunday nights, which had been dead when we arrived, started to become quite busy, the place full of couples enjoying a drink and a bite to eat. Within a few months of taking over we were already building a reputation as one of the better pubs in town and the weekly takings had risen from £120 to £800.

Meanwhile, the GPO had just started work on a new 20-storey headquarters right next door. The construction of the new building, complete with a large underground car park, threatened to weaken the foundations of The Railway Inn, so the GPO tried to buy it up with a view to demolishing it. The brewery, however, refused to sell, so the only option was to sink about eighty huge piles around the pub to shore it up.

The noise, mess and general inconvenience this created was clearly not very good for our now flourishing business. What's more, it meant that my Volvo 122S, my pride and joy, was permanently covered in a thick layer of mud and dust. Both these problems were eventually sorted out to our advantage in a rather unexpected way, but to explain exactly how this came about I first need to tell the story of how I came to acquire the Volvo and why it was so special to me.

It had belonged originally to Gerald Gold, financial director of the Birkenhead-based company that owned not only The Three Horse Shoes but also The Bear at Woodstock and The Bowler Hat Club in Birkenhead. On his regular trips down to London from Lancashire, Mr Gold would often break his journey either at Rugby or Woodstock, have dinner and then stay overnight before going on to London the next day. Whenever he came to The Three Horse Shoes, I would always make a point of cleaning his car for him. As a result, of course, he got to like me very much indeed!

In the restaurant one evening I overheard him telling his dinner companions that he would be going to the Motor Show at Earl's Court the next day to have a look at the latest Mercedes, which he was thinking of getting as a replacement for the Volvo. He explained to them that although he had only recently bought the 122S he had reluctantly decided he would have to sell it because his wife had taken against it.

As it happened, I had been looking around for a smarter car to replace the Capri before making my next visit back to Portugal and the Volvo 122S was at the top of my wish list, although well out of my price range unless I could find a cheap second-hand one. Jokingly I said: “So, Mr Gold, you have a Volvo 122S for sale? Fantastic! That’s just what I’m looking for.”

He simply smiled and said nothing but three weeks later he suddenly rang to tell me: “Lino, my Mercedes has just arrived. I am coming to The Three Horse Shoes tomorrow with my wife and she is going to bring the Volvo down for you. OK?” I went cold. I said: “Mr Gold, I could never afford to buy your car. I was only joking.”

He brushed all this aside. “Don’t worry, Lino,” he told me. “We own an HP company and I’ve got the finance sorted out for you. All you have to do is sign the papers. And, by the way, we’ve raised your wages by the exact amount of the monthly repayments so it’s not actually going to cost you a penny.”

I ended up keeping that Volvo for twenty-three years! And, as with all my cars, I made sure that it was always kept in immaculate condition, the paintwork buffed to a high sheen, the chrome gleaming and not a speck of dirt inside. I was not at all pleased, therefore, when, every time I now went to drive anywhere, I found it covered in dust from the pile-driving.

The contractors involved in the building work were Barratt’s of Birmingham and, as it happened, I knew Derek Barratt and his wife very well from the Westgate Arms, where they were among the regulars. I decided to ring them at home. Mrs Barratt answered the phone and sounded delighted to here from me. “Lino! Where the devil are you?” she cried, before I’d had a chance to say a word. “We miss you so much at the Westgate. What happened to you and when are you coming back?" I related the whole story, ending with the reason for my call. Could anything possibly be done to reduce the inconvenience caused by the building work, I wondered? She was very sympathetic and promised to get her husband to look into it.

The next thing we knew, an enormous billboard had gone up in a prime position outside the site announcing: 'Portuguese Couple Serving The Best Snacks In Leicester at The Railway Inn'. What's more, the Volvo was cleaned for me every day from then on.

Business improved yet further after this, but, even so, Augusta and I soon decided that we had no real long-term future there. Because of its location, the potential of the place was severely limited. More importantly, the routine it involved was starting to have an adverse effect on Peter's upbringing. We couldn't always leave him alone upstairs while we were working so, although he was only four years old, we had to let him come down to the bar where the customers would take great delight in trying to teach him how to play darts and dominoes. It was when he started picking up the odd swearword that we decided the time had maybe come to call it a day.

Mr Sabine, the man in charge of Ind Coope's tenancies, was desperate to keep us, offering us the pick of any one of the company's 10,000 pubs with the added incentive of £30,000 worth of free credit. It was an extremely tempting proposition, but I had now made up my mind that I would only ever put that much effort into a business again if it was a freehold property where I was working solely on my own behalf. Meanwhile, until the right opportunity came up, I decided that I would return to The Westgate.

I knew that my drive and enthusiasm had been badly missed, that Jack Spencer was keen to have me back and that, because of this, I would be in a position where I could negotiate better terms and conditions for myself. In addition, I insisted on going back not to the Town Bar but to the much more up-market cocktail bar. Not only would I be able to put my talents to better use there but I would also be picking up some handsome tips.

Not that I had lost any of my determination to set up on my own – far from it. If anything, the experience of running The Railway Inn had whetted my appetite even more because we had proved during our very short time there that we could make a success out of even the most unpromising situation. Just think what we could do with the right sort of place in a decent location!

In the meantime, we used the £800 that Augusta had managed to save out of the profits from the meals she had been serving at The Railway Inn to make the down payment on a very nice £3,000 house in Warwick, just a few minutes' walk from The Westgate itself. More importantly, with both of us working at the restaurant and with me making much better money, we felt we could now afford to send Peter to private school at Emscote Lawn.

Having had so little education myself, and being so very aware of its value, I was determined that Peter would have the best available. One of the reasons we never had more children was that, at the time, I could not have afforded to put more than one through private school.

Two years before Peter was conceived I had got chatting to one of the masters at Rugby school as I was serving him in the restaurant at The Three Horse Shoes. During the conversation he very kindly offered to show me around the place and I jumped at the opportunity. I was so impressed by what I saw there that even though I was still only a lowly waiter, earning less than £10-a-week, I made up my mind there and then that this was where I would one day send my own son. And, sure enough, I did just that! Driving Peter to Rugby and dropping him off at his boarding House on his very first day at what is one of the country's top public schools remains one of the proudest moments of my life. Amazingly, my granddaughter, Heather, and grandson James have both since followed him there to establish what I hope will become a family tradition.

Back at The Westgate, my re-appearance seemed to meet with the wholehearted approval of the regulars for whom my friendly, chatty approach had always provided a pleasant, easy-going contrast to the rather superior and occasionally quite intimidating manner adopted by Jack and Fred Spencer.

Jack, in particular, was undoubtedly a brilliant front man, parts of whose style I have copied and adapted for my own use. For instance, it was from watching him at work that I learned the importance of making a big fuss of the ladies. "Look after the ladies and the men will follow," he used to tell me.

With the people who mattered, he was magic. On the other hand, both he and his brother Fred were capable of treating customers whom they didn't know so well with that haughty disdain traditionally associated with a grand maitre d' of the old school. Their attitude seemed to suggest that you should feel grateful for the privilege of being allowed to eat in an establishment of which one food guide had written: "Don't bother to go if you don't have a Rolls Royce and a fur coat."

You would never have guessed from their rather snobbish demeanour that the two brothers actually came from a very poor background in London's East End. It was only many years later that Jack confided in me about this. Given my own lowly start in life I admired them all the more for this.

Stories of their perceived snootiness nevertheless abounded. For instance, anyone who couldn't quite make up his or her mind what to choose from the menu and who had the temerity to ask if any particular dish could be recommended would be bluntly informed that everything on the menu was perfect. It was the same with the wine. "I couldn't possibly suggest any particular wine because that would be unfair to the others on our list," Fred would say stiffly to anyone seeking a bit of guidance.

One regular customer, an extremely well-to-do local businessman, told me later how he had once taken a party of guests there for lunch, including one lady who was not especially hungry that day and who inquired very politely whether it might be possible to have just a portion of scampi and a few French fries. "If you want fish and chips, madam, I suggest you go elsewhere," she was told.

This was not untypical of the Spencer style, developed by Jack at the Savoy and Fred at the Caprice. They got away with it because there was no denying that both the food and the service generally were outstanding. Jack had brought the chef with him from the Savoy, via The Three Horse Shoes, and the waiters and kitchen staff were all trained to the highest West End standards.

At its peak in the late sixties and early seventies The Westgate was, without doubt, THE place to go in the Midlands. On Saturday evenings and Sunday lunchtimes especially, it would be buzzing, with the same local bigwigs at their usual tables week after week. And I went out of my way to make sure I got to know every one of them.

I would always make it my business to memorise the names not only of the customers themselves but also those of their children, their grandchildren and even their sons-and-daughters-in-law. I took a genuine interest in how every member of the family was getting on, what school the kids were at, what university they were going on to or what job they were doing. People were impressed by my memory for such details and would often sidle up and seek my advice when they couldn't quite recall the names of people whose faces they recognised. And, of course, it meant I was never at a loss for words with anyone. I always had something to chat to them about and that, in turn, helped to ensure that they always remembered me too.

In a way, I suppose you could say I was already networking long before that became a fashionable buzzword for the fairly cynical process of building up social and business contacts that might be useful in the future. There can certainly be no doubt that at The Three Horse Shoes and The Westgate I cultivated the sort of VIP customers who were to provide me with the loyal following that has supported me ever since. At the same time, I have always genuinely enjoyed making a fuss of my customers. I am, by nature, a friendly, gregarious type and I love my work. Augusta was always complaining that when we went on holiday I was never properly relaxed for long because I would soon start to miss the excitement of being front-of-house, meeting and greeting all my customers, many of whom have become close personal friends over the years.

They know that they can count on me for anything. It doesn't cost me a penny to make that extra little bit of effort and it gives me a great feeling of satisfaction to look after people in all sorts of special ways that I know will be appreciated. It is sometimes just a matter of being a good listener, lending a sympathetic ear to somebody with a problem who just wants to get it off his chest. Or it might be that, unasked, I can do somebody a little favour or kindness.

One example of just how much little things like that can mean concerns the late motor industry chief Sir George Harriman. He and his wife were regulars at both The Three Horse Shoes and The Westgate and they would often bring their Golden Retriever along, leaving him outside in the back of the car while they ate. And simply because I love dogs, I would always pop out and give him a bone or some other titbit from the kitchen. Of course, this dog soon grew to love me! After a while he got to recognise the route to the restaurant and would start getting excited long before the Harrimans turned into the car park.

Years later, when Sir George died, I was very touched to receive from Lady Harriman an 18-carat gold model of an Innocenti motor car that had been presented to her husband when he opened the Innocenti factory in Italy. She knew that I had an interest in cars and said that she had thought immediately that I was the right man to have this very special little memento.

Another indication of the sort of relationship I had developed with many of my customers concerned Mr and Mrs Barratt, a very wealthy couple from Stratford. They were celebrating Mr Barratt's birthday in the restaurant one evening and before they went in to dinner his wife presented him with a very expensive Lamy fountain pen as a gift. He was admiring it as I served them with their drinks

My parents, Manuel and Amelia, with Peter, aged four months, in Vinha in 1964.

Augusta with her family. Standing behind parents Manuel and Maria are (l to r) Francisco, Augusta, Jose, Maria Marques, Delfina and Maria Santos.

Me (seventh from the left) with the rest of the class at Paiágua. Note the hairstyle, already neatly groomed.

And me, at the age of twelve, wearing the uniform that went with my job at the café in Castelo Branco.

(Top): The house in Vinha where I was born and grew up. (Middle): Me and Augusta standing in front of the lean-to extension that I built onto the house for us to live in after we were married.

(Left): A view over the surrounding mountains. Vinha and Paiágua are located in the valley the far side of which can be seen immediately above my left shoulder.

Me (middle of the front row) during my National Service days.

Augusta, aged seventeen, outside her home in Paiágua and with me on our wedding day in 1957.

The two of us a year later.

Soldier boy: I always loved being in unform.

The Palacio de Seteais in Sintra.

Augusta outside the Adeja das Caves where she worked when she first joined me in Sintra.

Augusta and me with the Tahany family outside their home at Claybrooke Grange.

Augusta with young Peter Tahany, after whom we named our own son.

Augusta and me together on a day off in Leicester.

A Christmas party for the staff at The Three Horse Shoes, with me looking as if I'm the one who ate all the pies!

In my element, behind the bar at The Three Horse Shoes.

Proud dad with Peter, aged about one month.

and held it up for me to see, saying: "Just look at this, Lino. What a magnificent piece of engineering." I made an enthusiastic comment about what a lovely present it was whereupon Mrs Barratt smiled and said: "So, you like it do you, Lino?" "It's fantastic," I replied. "I've never seen anything like it." A few months later, on my own birthday, they came in again for a meal and much to my surprise she gave me an identical Lamy pen as a present.

Meanwhile, Augusta was also making a great impression on people with her own warm, friendly nature. She used to work in the cloakrooms and as she helped a lady on with her fur coat one evening she complimented her on the beautiful scent she was wearing. The next time that lady came in she gave Augusta a bottle of the same extremely expensive perfume. These were exactly the kind of people who were to support us so wonderfully well when we eventually got our own business.

My second spell at The Westgate lasted four years, from 1968 to 1972, and throughout that time I never stopped looking for a place in which to start up on my own. I even went as far as to go and knock on the door of guesthouses and B&Bs in the Warwick area, asking if there was any chance that they might be for sale. When Augusta's nephew, Eric, also came to work at the Westgate, I extended the search nationwide and we would spend our days off driving all round the country to look at likely places that I had seen advertised. Our travels took us as far afield as Fishguard and Dorset but most of the places we saw were not suitable and with those that did seem hopeful there would always be some other hitch, usually financial.

I didn't have much money of my own to invest at this time but several wealthy customers at The Westgate who knew what I was trying to do had offered to back me – although, when it came to the crunch, the money was not always forthcoming.

"If only you'd come to me last month before things got a bit tight," they would say, sucking in their cheeks and shaking their heads. After one or two possible deals had fallen through in this way I again started to get frustrated.

Then, eventually, I found exactly the sort of place I was looking for – a small nine-bedroom hotel in Leamington Spa called The Del Monte. The asking price was £30,000 of which I now had £12,000, this being the value of my house. I also had a backer, a businessman called Frank Sullivan, who had agreed to be my guarantor for a building society mortgage loan of £18,000.

With all the arrangements in place and contracts ready to be signed, my solicitor Tom Coleman, senior partner at Wright Hassall, suggested that we had better contact Mr Sullivan to make sure he wasn't going to let me down at the last moment as previous backers had done. When we called him, however, Frank was as good as his word. He agreed to speak immediately to his bank manager, authorising him to set up all the formalities, and added: "You don't need to bother about sending me any more details before we go ahead because I would back Lino anywhere, even if he opened up in the desert!"

Satisfied that the deal was to all intents cut and dried, I had actually started to move in some of our furniture when, on the very day that we were due to go in and sign the contract, the Building Society announced that their local search had revealed plans to build a roundabout on the site and that, as a result, they could not authorise the mortgage. Once again my dreams were in ruins. Totally devastated by this completely unexpected, last minute setback, Augusta and I sat in Tom Coleman's office in tears. As it turned out, the roundabout was never actually built.

Back at The Westgate I fretted over my bad luck. Then, at two o'clock one Sunday morning, after another busy Saturday night in the cocktail bar, a chance conversation with the last remaining customer changed everything. Bill Kendrick, multi-millionaire boss of the shipping company Sea Containers, was enjoying a final drink, chatting to me as I cleared up and prepared to close for the night. What future did I see for myself at The Westgate, he asked casually at one point. I told him how desperate I was for a place of my own, recounted the story of the Del Monte and explained that what I really wanted was a country pub.

"Really?" he said. "Well, it just so happens that I own a country pub which I'd be very happy to sell to you."

I nearly dropped the glass I was polishing. I had just three questions.

"Is it freehold?" I asked.

"Yes," he replied.

"And is it in Warwickshire?"

"It is."

"And how much do you want for it?"

"£30,000."

I hardly dared to believe my luck. I knew I would have no problem raising that sum of money because it was exactly what had only just been readily made available in principle for the Del Monte. I was so excited that I didn't even bother to bargain with him – a mistake, as it turned out, since I discovered much later that he had previously offered the place to somebody for just £22,000! As it was, I couldn't wait to take it off his hands. I held out my hand. "Mr Kendrick," I said, "the pub is mine. Now tell me, where is it exactly?"

Wherever it happened to be, I knew I could make a living at least as good as I was making at The Westgate – our experience at The Railway Inn had convinced me of that. The reason it was so important to me to be in Warwickshire was that by now I knew just about everybody in the county who was worth knowing and I was confident that if I needed help for anything, all I had to do was pick up the phone. I also had all these loyal customers who I was sure would support me as long as I wasn't too far away.

"It's in a village called Priors Hardwick," explained Mr Kendrick. He borrowed a scrap of paper and a biro and sketched me a little map. "You'd better go and have a look at it before you finally make up your mind," he added.

"I'll go tomorrow," I said excitedly. "But it won't make any difference. My mind is already made up."

Twelve days later the deal had been done and I was the very proud owner of The Butcher's Arms.

"PRIORS HARDWICK? WHERE'S THAT?"

Augusta's reaction on first catching sight of The Butcher's Arms was to burst into floods of tears.

I did my best to calm her down, pointing out that we weren't exactly seeing it in the best possible light. It was, after all, a cold, wet, grey Sunday evening at the end of November 1972 and we had had to drive round the village twice before we managed to locate the pub itself. "If we can't even find it with the help of a sketch map given to us by the owner, how are the customers ever going to find their way here," she wailed.

From the moment I had rushed back from The Westgate in a state of great excitement after my conversation with Bill Kendrick, Augusta had strongly suspected that she was once again going to be uprooted from the security of a comfortable home in which she felt very happy and secure and dumped in some remote spot in the middle of nowhere. What she saw when we eventually got there went way beyond even her worst fears.

An estate agent's particulars, had any existed, would undoubtedly have made it sound highly desirable. A quiet location in a picturesque village in the heart of the Warwickshire countryside; a rich history as a Royalist stronghold at the time of the Civil War; parts of the building dating back to 1375, making it older than the village church, a fact that reflected the common practice of building a hostelry first so the workmen would have somewhere to stay. I can imagine just how it might have been described. The reality, of course, didn't quite match the image this might have conjured up.

The place wasn't anything like it is today. The premises then consisted of just two pokey little bars plus a dark and dingy dining room, with space for no more than half-a-dozen cramped tables. At the back was a dilapidated kitchen, with a small domestic fridge and a four-ring cooker that was encrusted with what looked like years of grease and grime. Everything was filthy. The toilet was out in the yard, where a few near-derelict sheds were piled high with broken crates full of empty beer bottles and other accumulated rubbish. There was a rough paddock where the patio and garden is now and a narrow parking area at the front that was just one car deep, with a ditch running down the middle of it. The private accommodation upstairs was also very basic and badly in need of attention.

I have to admit that even I began to have slight misgivings as we looked around although, naturally, I didn't let on. It wasn't quite the pretty country pub I'd had in mind, but at the same time I was confident that we would be able to make a living out of it. And at least it would be a start. Augusta, however, remained totally unconvinced and extremely nervous about the whole proposition.

She always was, by nature, a bit of a worrier. Even when The Butcher's Arms became well-established and we were regularly catering for up to 1,000 customers a week, she would still get anxious every time we had a couple of quiet sessions in a row, fearing that the whole business was about to collapse. If we were overbooked she would fret about people having to wait a few minutes for a table, convinced that they would never come again. But however dubious she herself may have been about my grand schemes, she always loyally went along with my decisions in the end and then worked 110 per cent to make sure that everything was a success. She was always incredibly strong in that way, the rock on which the success of the entire business was founded.

As soon as we got back to Warwick, with Augusta wringing her hands and complaining tearfully every inch of the way that I must be out of my mind, I phoned Bill Kendrick to confirm that I definitely wanted to buy the place, adding that I would like to complete the deal as quickly as possible. To my horror, he then casually revealed that he was leaving for Australia in twelve days' time, would be away for six months and couldn't possibly do anything until he got back. "Trust me," he said. "The pub is yours. But we can't finalise the deal until I come back because Christmas is coming up and everybody is too busy to get things sorted out before I go."

Once again, I could see a golden opportunity slipping away. First thing on the Monday morning I went to see Tom Coleman and explained the situation. "There's no way we can get everything done before he goes away," he confirmed, glancing impatiently at his watch before adding: "I'm afraid I'm due in court in a few minutes so I haven't got time to discuss it now. Let's talk again next week." I begged him: "Mr Coleman, you don't understand. Mr Kendrick is going to Australia for six months and anything can happen. You never know, he might even die while he's out there. And then I will lose another place. So, please, you have to help me."

I had tears in my eyes. Tom was only too keenly aware of my terrible disappointment over the collapse of the Del Monte deal and I could sense that he felt I was owed a favour. His secretary, Jill, seeing how upset I was, also appealed to him: "Have you got another five minutes, Mr Coleman? Let's see what we can do."

He thought about it for a moment and then asked me if I had a telephone number for Bill Kendrick's solicitor, which I did. He rang him on the spot. "I've got Lino Pires here who is trying to buy The Butcher's Arms at Priors Hardwick from Mr Kendrick," he said. "Do you know anything about that?"

"I do," came the reply. "Mr Kendrick has just instructed me that the place has indeed been sold to Mr Pires."

"Excellent," said Tom. "In that case, I'd be grateful if you could draw up the contract up right away because I would like to send my clerk round to pick it up this afternoon."

He put the 'phone down and turned to me with a smile of triumph. "We will call a meeting with the building society on Thursday to see if they will still lend you the £18,000 they agreed for the Del Monte," he said. "And if they won't, then I will."

As Tom was a director of the building society in question and as I also happened to know the other two directors very well as regular customers at The Westgate, I didn't anticipate any real problems there. Sure enough, the loan was agreed and the entire deal was completed before Bill Kendrick left for Australia.

We moved in on New Year's Day, 1973. Augusta had a further moment of deep despair about what we were letting ourselves in for when the removal van, in which she was travelling with Peter while I went on ahead in the car, first got lost and then nearly ran aground on the narrow little hump-back bridge over the canal at Marston Doles. Once again, Augusta was convinced that none of my customers from The Westgate would ever dream of venturing so far out into the sticks.

Meanwhile, my announcement that I was again leaving to set up on my own had not gone down too well with Jack Spencer. Jack always seemed to take it as a personal insult if any of his staff left him voluntarily and, as a rule, you would never be allowed to darken his doorstep again.

In that respect, he got almost as good as he gave from at least one of his more illustrious former employees. Among the Italian waiters he had working for him at The Three Horse Shoes when I first arrived there was Franco Taruschio. Franco left in 1963 to open The Walnut Tree in Abergavenny, which, despite its location even further off the beaten track than The Butcher's Arms, went on to become one of the most celebrated restaurants in Britain. Some years later Jack was taken there for lunch by a friend, only to find when they got there that Franco, still harbouring bitter memories of what he considered to be the overbearing way in which he and his fellow Italians had been treated at The Three Horse Shoes, was reluctant to let him in. He relented in the end but not without making his feelings very clear.

Very much one of the old school, Jack could certainly be a very hard taskmaster although I, personally, had no complaints on that particular score. As far as I was concerned, he was tough but fair and I had tremendous respect for him. He was, after all, the man largely responsible for starting a restaurant revolution in the

Midlands, introducing sophisticated West End standards to the provinces for the first time. He gave me my start, something for which I shall always be grateful, and it is probably true to say that he taught me just about everything I know.

At The Three Horse Shoes and then The Westgate I had deliberately gone out of my way to win his trust, sensing, with an eye to the future, that I had a lot to gain from getting into his good books. Consequently, my attitude towards him was that nothing was ever too much trouble and, in addition, I used to do him all sorts of little favours. I would regularly wash and polish his car in my spare time and Augusta would bake him a cake every weekend without fail. When he commented one day on how immaculately my shirt had been laundered by Augusta, I got her to do his as well and for the next twelve years she hand-washed and ironed not only his shirts but his brother's as well, often as many as fifteen a week altogether. And for this she was paid just a few shillings a week extra.

Gradually, over the years, Jack and I developed a grudging mutual respect. He liked my style because he could see how well it was going down with the customers and he also learned to trust my judgement about the way certain things could be improved. I kept him well posted about what was going on 'below stairs', and warned him in advance whenever I could see potential trouble brewing. It was because of all this that he made an exception in my case and welcomed me back after my earlier 'defection' to the Railway Inn. But even I wasn't going to be allowed to get away with things so easily the second time around.

Once the deal with Bill Kendrick had been signed and sealed I was keen to get started at The Butcher's Arms as quickly as possible, so I came to an arrangement with Jack whereby we agreed that instead of working out my notice in the normal way I would continue to come in at lunchtimes only, for as long as it took me to train up my successor in the cocktail bar.

This seemed to be in the best interests of both of us. As far as I was concerned, it meant that I would be guaranteed a bit of income during the early weeks at Priors Hardwick when I wasn't sure how busy we were going to be and feared that I might be struggling for a while to pay both the mortgage and Peter's school fees at Emscote Lawn. From Jack's point of view, it saved him the trouble of having to go out and find a ready-trained barman to take over from me.

The arrangement lasted for just three days. During that time Jack never once mentioned The Butcher's Arms or even deigned to ask me how things were going. Not a word. Looking back now, I suspect that quite apart from being irritated with me for leaving him again, he was probably a bit jealous of my new venture. At the time, however, I was very hurt by his apparent lack of interest. Then, on the fourth day, he suddenly snapped at me: "Lino, this isn't going to work – you will have to be here in the evenings as well."

Knowing that there was no way that I could possibly leave Augusta to cope on her own at Priors Hardwick, I reacted angrily. I said: "Mr Spencer, you are breaking our agreement. As far as I am concerned, that's it. I'm leaving now." And, in the middle of lunch, in front of a hundred people in the crowded dining room, I took off my little red uniform jacket, handed it over to him and walked out.

A week later he rang The Butcher's Arms at a time when he knew I wouldn't be around and spoke to Augusta. He said he was sorry that we had parted on such bad terms, adding that he thought I might also be owed some holiday pay. Augusta was soon in tears. She told him: "Mr Spencer, Lino would be so pleased to see you here – why not come over to see us so we can get everything sorted out?" But he didn't come and we heard nothing more.

It was another twelve years before he was at last persuaded to visit The Butcher's Arms by our mutual friend Harry Webster, one of my oldest and most valued customers, now sadly no longer with us. Harry, the former Chief Engineer at Standard Triumph, was a legendary figure in the car industry, famously responsible for designing the Triumph Herald, the Stag and also the TR series of sports cars along with the Italian stylist Giovanni Michelotti, some of whose original sketches can be seen on the wall of the restaurant. I had first got to know Harry when I served him at The Three Horse Shoes and then at The Westgate Arms. Over the years, he and his wife, Peggy, became not only our most loyal customers, coming in for lunch every Sunday, almost without fail. They also became really close friends, holidaying with us at our villa in Portugal on several occasions. At the same time, they were equally friendly with Jack and his wife and, in the end, managed to convince them that a proper reconciliation was long overdue.

Unlike Franco, I welcomed my former boss with open arms. From then on he came in regularly right up until his death and I made a point of rarely charging him a penny. He said to Augusta once, shaking his head: "I don't deserve this from Lino after I treated him so inconsiderately when he left The Westgate." Augusta smiled and told him: "Well, Lino is like that."

Those very early days at The Butcher's Arms were pretty frantic, but I remember them as some of the most exciting of my life. We were working harder than we had ever worked before but the great thing was that we were doing it for ourselves at last and not for anybody else. Every time I heard that till ring it was like music to my ears – and it was soon ringing with encouraging frequency.

Our arrival in the village had been greeted with considerable curiosity, not least because word had got round in advance that the pub was being taken over by a black couple! It hadn't taken long for local gossip and a few Chinese whispers to transform a 'foreign' couple into a 'black' couple. One of the first things I did on the morning after we moved in was to go round to the little village post office to introduce myself to post mistress Mary Winn. Everybody used the post office and I knew that this would be by far the quickest way to spread the news that The Butcher's Arms was now under the management of Lino and Augusta Pires, who, as Mary then kindly informed everybody, were actually 'a very nice, friendly Portuguese couple'.

The bar was busier than normal that lunchtime as the locals came in to check us out. Among them was farm worker Malcolm Reynolds, a wonderful old village character who later came to work for us part-time as a gardener and odd job man and was with us for many years. Having lived in Priors Hardwick for well over fifty years, Malcolm could remember back to the days when the place was lit by oil lamps and a formidable-sounding landlady called Ada Gee would sometimes have to be summoned from her garden to pull you a pint when things were quiet.

Sitting in a corner of our little public bar, with old photographs on the wall of the 1950s village football team that included a youthful Malcolm, he would be full of entertaining reminiscences about characters like his friend Len Mole, who habitually used to take the poker out of the fire and stick it in his pint to warm it up. A Coldstream Guardsman during the war, Malcolm's exploits included guarding Rudolph Hess, fighting alongside a Sergeant Major who won the VC at Salerno and finding himself less than two miles from Mount Vesuvius when it erupted in 1944. After that, life down on the farm in Priors Hardwick must have seemed very dull.

On the evening of our first day, Nat Sherwood, the father of show jumper Oliver Sherwood, became our very first restaurant customer. It was the local Young Farmers, however, who really ensured that we got off to a flying start. Farming was a flourishing industry in those days and the Young Farmers were a large and very lively bunch, with enormous appetites and plenty of money to spend. They soon got a taste for Augusta's gammon and eggs, steaks and casseroles and they loved what was, in those days, our rather liberal interpretation of the licensing laws!

During my years at The Three Horse Shoes and The Westgate I had got to know everybody who was anybody in Warwickshire, one reason why I had been so keen to make sure when I did eventually get a place of my own that it was located within the county boundary. Among the valuable contacts I had made was a senior police officer who had once revealed to me that the police were not too concerned about after-hours drinking in country pubs as long as it was carried on discreetly and there wasn't any trouble.

With a well-behaved bunch of hefty, rugby-playing Young Farmers in the bar, many of them built like the side of a barn, any troublesome and undesirable outside elements were very quickly discouraged and we never experienced the slightest problem. In fact, off-duty policemen themselves would often drop in for an after-hours pint. At the same time we were soon doing a roaring trade in food, dishing up steaks until midnight and even later if required.

The only person who was not always entirely happy with this arrangement was poor Augusta, who was regularly to be found slaving away in the kitchen until all hours. What used to upset her most of all was the situation where, at the very moment when she had just finally turned everything off and tidied up at what she thought was the end of another long, hard day, I would come through with yet another order. She never actually threw anything at me but she came close to it on many occasions, complaining bitterly about the fact that I just couldn't bring myself to say no to anyone.

"It's all very well for you out there in the front, being charming to everybody who comes in and going 'kissy-kissy' with all the beautiful girls," she would cry. "You forget that out here at the back it is me who is doing all the hard work!"

I nicknamed her the Mona Lisa – because she used to moan a lot! But, of course, she had every right to get fed up with me, especially in those early months when she was alone in the kitchen. We were not, at that stage, in a position to be able to afford either proper equipment or extra staff to help her out and as our reputation for good food began to spread rapidly she was soon struggling to keep pace with demand.

There was no respite for her, especially once we started doing Sunday lunches. We used to get quite a few people coming in for pre-lunch drinks on Sunday, but they would always then go home to eat until one day I got Augusta to cook a big roast, which I made a point of bringing out to show everybody in the bar as they were getting ready to leave, saying: "Look, this is what Augusta and I are having for lunch. Would anybody else like to try some?" It looked so mouth-watering that I knew people would find it hard to resist. That was how Patrick Englert and his wife, Anne, were tempted to become our first Sunday lunch customers and before too long Augusta found herself cooking anything up to seventy or eighty lunches every Sunday on her one tiny stove. At the end of the day her arms would be aching so much from the cutting and chopping and peeling and mixing that she would hardly be able to lift them.

At the same time, my muscles were equally sore from helping out during every spare moment of the day and night with the building work that I had begun almost as soon as we moved in and which has continued on and off ever since. A Good Food Guide entry once included the comment that "Lino Pires seems to change The Butcher's Arms almost as often as his homeland changes its Government", a reference to the period of political instability in Portugal following the revolution in 1974.

For the first few years the place resembled a permanent building site as we set about improving and expanding the premises. The first priority was to move the toilets inside, followed by the enlargement of the main bar and the dining room, the modernisation of the kitchen, the building of store rooms and a laundry at the back and the conversion of the sheds outside into staff accommodation.

In Colin Amor I was lucky enough to find a wonderful local builder who has been involved in every one of the many extensions that have subsequently been added, including the new conservatory that was completed in 2001. In those early years I used to work alongside Colin as his unpaid labourer and customers arriving early for lunch would often find me busy mixing concrete or wheeling barrow loads of sand and cement around the place.

While all this was going on we never once missed a session. Colin would often move in with a team of workmen as the last customers were leaving after Sunday lunch and would then work through the night to get the next stage of a job finished in time for us to open as usual for lunch on Monday. Even when there was a bit of disruption people never seemed to mind. They would actually get quite caught up in all the excitement, asking: "What are you up to now, Lino? I can't wait to come back and see it all finished!"

In my initial enthusiasm to get on with the conversion as quickly as possible, I inadvertently overlooked the small matter of planning permission. The majority of people in the village were delighted at the prospect of having a thriving pub restaurant in their midst but, inevitably, there were one or two diehards who, fearing that their peace and quiet might be disturbed, were not so keen on the idea of breathing new life into what was then a dying community. As we began knocking through walls to enlarge the bar and a growing mountain of rubble appeared in the back yard, some anonymous busybody reported me to the police for going ahead without the necessary permission.

Fortunately, the officer who logged the complaint was a good customer and an old friend of mine who immediately rang to tip me off. He explained that although planning permission was not normally needed for internal alterations, a special magistrate's licence was required for licensed premises and that maybe I should see if I could get it sorted out quickly before an official check was set in motion.

My architect and I hurriedly presented the plans as if the work had not yet been started and the necessary licence was duly granted. People told me: "Lino, only you could have got away with it." It was a bit the same with the car park. When we arrived it was a fraction of the size it is now and had a large ditch running down the middle so that there just wasn't enough room for all the cars. I couldn't get formal permission to build a car park as such so I simply put drainage pipes in the ditch, filled it in and covered it over to create the large parking area we have now. I just didn't immediately put a sign up saying Car Park.

Augusta's fears that Westgate customers would not come to such an out-of-the-way place quickly proved unfounded as a steady stream of very smart cars began to be seen making their way rather uncertainly along the narrow lanes leading into the village. Local people soon got so used to being hailed from passing Jaguars and Rolls Royces by drivers asking politely for directions to The Butcher's Arms that they would have their answers ready even before the electric window had been lowered.

In our little bar and dining room the Young Farmers suddenly found themselves rubbing shoulders on a regular basis with some of the leading Midlands businessmen and industrialists of the day. Sir William Lyons of Jaguar, construction magnates Sir Charles Turriff and John Barratt, jeweller George Pragnell, Donington Park owner Tom Wheatcroft, millionaire businessman Eddie Large, top car designer Harry Webster – they all came to see how we were getting on, liked what they saw and spread the good word.

Although Jack Spencer stayed away, his son Roy, who, by now had joined him at The Westgate, did drop in to check out what the fuss was all about – and was seemingly unimpressed. He happened to be in the restaurant one evening when Eddie Large and his wife Rita were also there, Eddie in expansive mood as usual, smoking a big cigar and having a great time. A week later, back at The Westgate, Eddie had reason to complain about something that he felt wasn't quite up to scratch and Roy was indignant. "I don't understand what you are complaining about, Mr Large," he said. "I saw you last week at The Butcher's Arms, which has very little to offer compared with what we have here, and you seemed perfectly happy."

"Roy, you miss the point," explained Eddie patiently. "When I go to Lino's place I always get more than I expect. When I come to The Westgate, on the other hand, I always expect a lot – and tonight I didn't quite get it."

It was not too long after this that The Westgate started to go into a gradual decline. Roy's arrival had coincided with Fred Spencer moving to The Three Horse Shoes and with Jack himself apparently content to take more of a back seat and to leave the running of the place to his son, it seemed to lose some of its old magic. When that happens, it is surprising how quickly even the most fashionable restaurants can fall out of favour.

Roy, by all accounts, simply did not have his father's special genius as a restaurateur. Whatever the reason, there was soon a fairly steady drift of clientele from The Westgate to The Butcher's Arms, including some very valuable business account customers. This general exodus was hastened by the introduction of one or two changes that I found hard to understand from a business point of view.

First came the decision to stop serving Sunday lunch. Sunday lunch at The Westgate had become something of an institution, hugely popular with the regular customers, many of whom used to go there with their families almost every weekend. Its discontinuation upset a lot of people. At the same time, quite a bit of money was invested in adding some hotel rooms and, again, I thought this was a mistake. Once you have bedrooms, you need a whole lot of extra staff to run them and service them. Taking into account all the other complications involved, this is the main reason why I have never been tempted to have rooms at The Butcher's Arms, even though several people have suggested it over the years. Better, in my view, to concentrate exclusively on the restaurant side and not take your eye off the ball.

The Westgate kept going until the late eighties but it seemed to me and many other people that it was never quite the same again once Jack Spencer was no longer in full control. As its reputation faded, it was eventually sold to a consortium that tried, without success, to revive it and it finally closed down altogether in 1990.

There was a sad little postscript to all this. When Jack Spencer died a few years later I naturally wanted to attend his funeral. I arranged to go with Harry Webster, who had been a great friend of his, and also with my head waiter Steve Syvret, who, like me, had worked under Jack at The Westgate for a time. However, when we arrived at the crematorium we were surprised to be turned away by Roy who made it clear in no uncertain terms that we were not welcome. Later, after I and one or two others had let it be known how upset we were at not being allowed to pay our respects, he did relent and we were all invited to a memorial service in Warwick.

It gave me no great pleasure to watch the decline and eventual disappearance of The Westgate but there is no doubt that we benefited from it at The Butcher's Arms. The more The Westgate went downhill, the more we found ourselves on the up and up as customers started looking around for an alternative. For once, it seemed, my timing had been spot on.

STARS AND CARS

Cashing up at the end of our first day at The Butcher's Arms we found that we had taken the princely sum of £17. I remember the exact figure very clearly because it was precisely what I had previously been paid for a whole week of hard labour at The Westgate. From that moment on, I never really doubted that we were going to make a success of our new venture.

In the year before we took over the total takings had been £2,700; in our first full year they topped £20,000. As the business continued to expand rapidly we began taking on permanent staff to help us out. First to arrive was Augusta's nephew Eric. On my recommendation, Eric had been brought over from Portugal by Jack Spencer the previous year, aged eighteen, to work as a waiter at The Westgate and he then followed us to The Butcher's Arms at Easter, 1973. He was joined later by his brother Joseph, who had been working at The Bowler Hat Club in Birkenhead, again on my recommendation, and who had then gone to France for a short time before coming to us.

My cousin, Adriano, and his wife, Laurinda, then came over from Portugal and moved into a small bungalow opposite the church that we were renting. Adriano was to be with us as a waiter for twenty-three years, a lovely, lovely man who became a great favourite with all our regular customers and who will always be remembered with great affection. Sadly, he died shortly after leaving us in 1998 to return home to Portugal.

The main reason we kept sending back to Portugal for staff was that nobody in this country was interested in becoming a professional waiter in those days. It was still looked down on then as the sort of job that was fit only for 'bloody foreigners'. As it happened, I was very happy to be able provide opportunities for people back home, especially old friends and members of my extended family who found themselves in the same position that I had once been in myself, desperate to get away and to find a better future for themselves.

Growing up in Vinha, my two best pals had been brothers Joao and Lorenso Simao, whose father owned a big farm in the neighbouring village of Silvosa where I and my family regularly found work. As teenagers, Lorenso and I, in particular, would go everywhere together. He had learned to play the guitar and, as a result, was much in demand at fiestas and parties where he would become a centre of attention, very useful when it came to chatting up the girls! We all lost touch for a while after I moved to England but the two brothers both got married and settled down in the area – and each had sons who ended up coming to work for me at The Butcher's Arms. Joao's son, Francisco, known to everybody as Simon, became our head chef and was with us for twenty-seven years altogether before leaving to start up on his own, while Lorenso's son Alberto, also a chef, had been with us for more than twenty years when he eventually left in 2009.

Until Simon arrived late in 1975, Augusta did all the cooking herself, an incredible effort given the fact that, by then, we were very busy all the time with up to a hundred covers every day. Businessman Fred Ward and his wife were among the early regulars who also became good friends and they took pity on Augusta to such an extent that Mrs Ward would insist on getting up from the table at the end of the evening to go into the kitchen and help her with the washing up while Fred, who used to give me a hand with the accounts, eventually took me on one side and gave me quite a severe lecture about how I needed to take better care of my wife.

"You're killing her with work, Lino," he warned me anxiously. "Money isn't everything. Why not let her take it a bit easier." I told him: "Fred, hard work never killed anybody. It makes your muscles ache but it doesn't kill you. You mustn't worry about Augusta. Nobody could ever love her more than I do, nobody values and appreciates what she does more than I do and nobody will ever come between us. She is the most wonderful, loyal wife and I rely on her completely. I know she complains about me but, in the end, she wouldn't want me to do things any differently. She may appear to be shy and a little lacking in self-confidence but she is stronger than you think and just as determined as I am to make a success of the business."

There is no doubt that Augusta deserved much of the credit for establishing the early and lasting reputation of The Butcher's Arms as the best restaurant in Warwickshire, regarded by a highly discerning clientele as being every bit as good, if not better, than The Three Horse Shoes and The Westgate had been at their peak. This achievement was made all the more remarkable by the fact that she managed it without any formal training whatsoever.

Like any Portuguese peasant girl of her generation, she had learned the basics of cooking at her mother's knee, in circumstances that called for great skill and ingenuity in making the most of extremely limited ingredients.

When we first arrived in this country and started working for the Tahany family, Augusta was quite shocked by the blandness of much British home cooking and found that her soups, stews, casseroles and, in particular, her marinated chicken and chicken with chilli – all prepared using simple, traditional Portuguese recipes – were an instant sensation.

Later, she picked up a great deal simply from watching what was going on in the kitchens at The Three Horse Shoes and The Westgate, even though she herself never actually cooked at either place. Thrown in at the deep end at The Butcher's Arms, she started with a few fairly straightforward dishes, mostly gammon, steaks, chicken and scampi. Then, as the restaurant rapidly expanded and the menu became more extensive and sophisticated, she simply worked from the classic cookbooks, learning as she went along.

She just had a fantastic natural talent. She taught Simon to cook from scratch before he eventually took over as head chef and, although he became very good indeed, there were still some dishes that he was never able to do quite as well as Augusta herself. Her sweets and desserts were a speciality and regulars will tell you that her bread-and-butter pudding and her profiteroles, in particular, were quite distinctive. They would say that they could always tell instantly whether they had been made by Augusta herself or by one of the other chefs. When it came to the bread-and-butter pudding, Terri McGregor, in charge of the sweet trolley for more than thirty years now, insists that she could tell at a glance whether it was one of Augusta's. "Hers always looked so wonderfully light, almost like a souffle," says Terri.

Our policy at The Butcher's Arms has always been to concentrate on the idea of simple food, well cooked and well presented. We don't pretend to be offering haute cuisine and we've never been interested in nouvelle cuisine or any other passing food fads. The menu doesn't change that often – although we did recently add Ostrich steaks, to prove, as it were, that our heads are not stuck in the sand in this respect – and our regular customers, many of whom have been coming for thirty years now, seem to prefer things that way. Some will even go to the lengths of reserving a portion of their "usual" in advance to guard against a run on some of the more popular dishes.

I suspect that there may be quite a few stalwarts who have tried everything on the menu at some time or other over the years, but there is only one man, as far as I know, who can claim to have gone through the card in a single week. Michael Rosenberg, a retired financier, planned it all meticulously. A very wealthy man, accustomed to cruising the world in the QE2, Michael hired the most luxurious and well-appointed canal barge he could find and moored it down by the lock at Marston Doles. He and his wife, Jocelyn, then proceeded to come up to the restaurant for lunch and dinner every day for a week, driving up in the splendid Aston Martin V8 Volante that I later bought from him. By the end of his marathon performance, Michael had, indeed, tried every dish on offer, including starters, main courses and desserts. We had to admire his stamina but were not especially surprised when he didn't re-appear for a while afterwards! His favourite dishes, incidentally, turned out to be langoustines in brandy sauce, Chateaubriand and chocolate profiteroles.

The quality of the food is obviously the basic criterion on which any restaurant is judged, but that is not the only secret of our success at The Butcher's Arms. Right from the start, we set out to create a special sort of atmosphere. And that's where I come in, I suppose. I can barely boil an egg, I hate paperwork and I'm rather clumsy and impractical when it comes to improving the décor. Peter himself dines out on stories of the near-disasters I have caused behind the scenes over the years with some of my D-I-Y ventures. But I do know how to look after people. I know how to make them relax and feel at home and how to make sure that they go away already looking forward to their next visit.

I have to admit that sometimes I will quite deliberately go a bit over the top, especially with showbiz personalities. "Wow! I have watched you on the television so many times and I've read so much about you but never in my lifetime did I ever think I would meet you. Fantastic! It is such a privilege to have you here. My staff will drop everything to serve you." That's the sort of thing. A little bit of bullshit never did anyone any harm in my business!

At the same time, it is not something you can ever carry off if you are totally cynical. You have to mean it and, mostly, I do. I am genuinely pleased to see my customers, I love the excitement of playing host to a big star name and I positively look forward to being on duty at 12 o'clock and 7.00pm each day, all dressed up and ready to meet and greet everybody as they arrive. Augusta used to tell me off when we were on holiday because I would get restless after two or three days without the excitement of playing host to my customers. People sometimes ask me if I get fed up with the fact that our busy six-nights-a-week routine leaves so little time to socialise but I tell them: "I am not missing out. Why would I worry about not being able to go to the odd party when I have a party here in my restaurant every night."

I get to meet all sorts of interesting people and, no matter who they might be, I am never at a loss for words. As far as I can recall there has only ever been one occasion when I have been left absolutely speechless and that was not in the restaurant. It was during a holiday in Portugal with Harry and Peggy Webster when we all went to see the excellent cabaret at the casino in Estoril and made the big mistake of sitting in the front row. The show included a ventriloquist who called me up on stage at one point in his act to become his human dummy. As he slipped his hand up the back of my jacket he whispered in my ear: "Every time I pinch you I want you to open and shut your mouth." Of course, he soon had me seeming to say all sorts of ridiculous things and, out in the audience, I could see Harry, Peggy and Augusta all falling about in their seats, helpless with laughter. Harry always used to insist that it was the funniest thing he'd ever seen in his life.

Normally, of course, you can't shut me up. I'll chat away to anyone and I'm just as much at ease with a duke as I am with a dustman. Or even, come to that, a bit of a crook. One of the more colourful characters among our early customers was the notorious burglar-turned-artist Jago Stone. Jago had first taken up painting in prison, winning a prize for prison art while doing time for a series of offences. As a burglar, he used to specialise in stealing antique silver from churches, sometimes disguised as a cleric and even, on one well-publicised occasion, as a monk! That, at least, showed a bit of style.

We got to know him quite well when he settled for a while just up the road in Hellidon, making an honest living for himself at last by going around painting pictures of large houses in the area and selling them to the owners. He would be in the bar at The Butcher's Arms almost every night at this time and he was always very entertaining company. I once said to him, half-jokingly: "I would never dream of buying any silver for this place, Jago, because it's bound to be nicked!" And he replied, deadpan: "Lino, you're very wise."

He looked like a stage villain, with his handlebar moustache, but he was, if anything, a lovable rogue, with a great sense of humour. He even wrote a best-selling book called The Burglar's Bedside Companion! And he told us a very amusing story about how, when he eventually came out of prison, the police had asked him where he had hidden all the silver he had stolen, none of which had ever been recovered. He obligingly took them all the way to Birmingham, led them to a multi-storey block of flats and told them innocently: "It must be under there somewhere. I buried it all on this site but these flats have gone up since then." He swore to us that this was the truth but he was always telling tales like that and you could never be quite sure.

Despite his rather scruffy appearance, Jago was a great ladies man. Women found him totally irresistible and he could have all the crumpet he wanted. He was involved in all sorts of scandals, with one man even reported to have paid him £500 to stay away from his wife.

The last we heard of him was some time after he had moved away from Hellidon and we picked up the Sunday papers to find that he had hit the headlines yet again, marrying a young woman in the face of bitter opposition from her well-to-do family only to then ditch her just hours later. Apparently, he and his new bride were being driven home from the wedding reception when he suddenly ordered the driver of the limousine to stop at a telephone box, rang his ex-wife and asked her to come and pick him up, saying that he'd made a mistake and wanted to go back to her.

I still have one of his pictures up on the wall in the restaurant. It is there alongside the signed photographs of some of the celebrity customers we have served over the years, a tradition that began with cricketing hero Ian Botham. Ian was at the very peak of his rumbustious career when he came here to open an exhibition of watercolours by an artist friend of his called J.H. Hurst, whose view of The Butcher's Arms from across the big, showpiece garden that we used to have at the back here can be seen hanging in the coffee lounge. It just so happened that on that very morning Ian was in the news yet again for some reason and so we were deluged with Press and TV reporters, all chasing him for a comment, with the result that Mr Hurst ended up getting a lot more publicity than he bargained for. It certainly didn't do us any harm, either.

Despite all the unwelcome media attention, Ian was absolutely charming and extremely relaxed, and his wife, Kath, was equally delightful. I had a long chat with her about Portugal, where the two of them were planning to go on holiday, and I was able to recommend several places that I felt they should make a point of visiting. Later, she wrote me a lovely letter to tell me what a great time they'd had. Ian's manager, meanwhile, had given me a signed photograph, which we put up on the wall, and that's how the collection got started.

Our gallery now includes everyone one from American astronaut Tom Stafford to Selina Scott and from Stirling Moss to Bobby Davro. Actors and actresses such as John Bowe, Peter Jeffrey, Susan George and Joanna Lumley are up there alongside pop stars Slade and The Moody Blues' Graeme Edge, television personalities Kay Alexander, Richard Madeley and Judy Finnegan and soccer pundits Jimmy Hill and Ron Atkinson. But the majority of those featured happen to have been involved with the world of motorsport, a connection that can be traced right back to a couple of our earliest and dearest customers.

Former Le Mans star David Hobbs, now a highly-respected Formula 1 racing commentator for satellite television, and one-time RAC Rally winner Tony Mason, later a popular presenter on BBC TV's Top Gear, both lived locally for many years – although David is now based in America – and between them they were responsible for introducing scores of top drivers and other personalities to The Butcher's Arms, helping to establish us as what has been described as 'the social hub of the motorsport industry' in an area centred on Silverstone.

Other leading figures from the worlds of rallying and Formula 1 who use the restaurant on a regular basis both privately and for business entertaining include British and World Championship-winning rally team boss David Sutton, Mitsubishi's Andrew Cowan – twice winner of the London-Sydney Marathon Rally in his days as a driver – and David Richards, founder and chairman of Prodrive, owner of Aston Martin, former team principal with both the BAR and Benetton Formula 1 racing teams and the man responsible for the huge success of the Subaru world rally team at its peak. One way and another, it's perhaps not surprising that the dining room here sometimes seems like an annexe to the paddock at Silverstone.

David and Margaret Hobbs were among the first through the door when we opened in 1973 and have been using the place like a canteen ever since, becoming close family friends along the way. They are a wonderfully entertaining couple, but dangerous company for anyone looking for an early night!

Margaret, with her bubbly, fun-loving personality, is up for anything – she celebrated her 50th birthday by climbing Everest with a couple of girlfriends and then wrote a highly-acclaimed book about the whole adventure – while David, with his laid-back manner, droll sense of humour and talent for mimicry, is renowned as a hilarious after-dinner speaker, much in demand for friends' wedding anniversaries and big birthday parties, quite a few of which seem to have been held at The Butcher's Arms.

During a very successful racing career that spanned more than three decades and included a Championship victory and a near-record number of individual race wins at Formula 5000 level, three third-place finishes at Le Mans and third place in his Formula 1 debut in 1966, David got to know just about everybody who is anybody in motor sport and has a fund of funny stories.

His wicked take-off of former World Champion Nigel Mansell is one party piece that invariably brings the house down but my favourite David Hobbs anecdote is one he tells against himself. At

Silverstone for the British Grand Prix a few years ago he bumped into his old friend Jackie Stewart, who was strolling around the paddock with two small boys in tow. "Hello there, Jackie," drawled David. "I see you've got the brats with you." At this, two rather large gentlemen in dark glasses who were walking just behind Jackie stiffened slightly. The 'brats' it turned out were none other than Prince William and Prince Harry, enjoying a day out at the races with Jackie, a close friend of the Royal Family.

David and Margaret are among the select few who have come for lunch at The Butcher's Arms and stayed on for dinner, arriving at noon and not finally leaving until 10.30pm, a feat that requires considerable stamina. David is helped in this respect by having a constitution like an ox and an ability to nod off during a meal and then awake refreshed. My son Peter tells of a classic example when they were in Portugal together for the Portuguese Grand Prix. Our villa near Sintra is not far from the Estoril circuit and as a motor racing fan Peter often used to go over for the event, until it was dropped from the Grand Prix programme after the owners of the circuit sadly failed to carry out the required safety improvements and lost their FIA licence.

On this particular occasion David was taking a party of people out to dinner but at some point between the sweet and the coffee he was seen to have fallen into a familiar pose, arms folded, chin resting on his chest, eyes closed. Everyone else carried on regardless around him until, some time after midnight and with the restaurant starting to empty, Peter himself began to feel decidedly weary and was more than ready to call it a day. He was therefore quite relieved when David suddenly snapped awake and raised an arm to attract the waiter, as if about to call for the bill. Instead, to Peter's horror, he simply ordered two more bottles of port!

I myself have been involved in one or two memorable off-duty sessions with David in the days when we would go off with a couple of other friends from time to time for 'awayday' lunches at various top restaurants around the country. We once went all the way to the Sharrow Bay Hotel on Lake Windermere just for lunch. As a former professional racing driver, David would always take the wheel on these occasions, which perhaps explains why we were able to go so far and yet still get back to Priors Hardwick in time for me to be on duty at The Butcher's Arms as the first customers started arriving for dinner.

I remember, in particular, a trip to The Walnut Tree at Abergavenny. With us on that occasion were Brian Cripps, who had a BMW dealership at Kibworth in Leicestershire, and Coventry businessman Roy Meakins, another regular at The Butcher's Arms. Brian had organised the biggest BMW he could lay his hands on, which David proceeded to put through its paces in a fashion that would have impressed even the likes of Richard Burns and Colin McRae.

Arriving back slightly green about the gills, Roy Meakins commented that he thought he had probably just experienced G-Forces greater than those to which Neil Armstrong had been subjected in the Apollo moon rocket. He wondered whether anybody had noticed a re-entry glow on the car! David, meanwhile, was stretched out asleep on the bench seat in the bar.

Tony Mason, who made history in 1972 when he and Roger Clark became the first-ever British crew to win the RAC Rally, started coming to The Butcher's Arms shortly after David. He and his wife, Sue, had just moved to Moreton Pinkney to set up a small motor accessories business in Woodford Halse and Tony often used to nip in at lunchtime. He was always in such a rush that he never seemed to have time to sit down for a proper lunch and although we don't do bar snacks as a rule we used to make an exception for him just because he was such a lovely chap, sitting him in the corner of the public bar with a bit of pate and toast. In return, he would organise tickets to Silverstone for Peter through his contacts.

He repaid us even more handsomely once he got the job on Top Gear. From then on he would make a point of bringing in all his VIP friends from the worlds of television and motorsport. He even arranged to film some of his television interviews here, with the restaurant in the background, providing us with some wonderful publicity.

Apart from that, it was a great thrill for Peter and I, both motor sport fans, to have these great personalities coming in all the time. Stirling Moss, Jackie Stewart, Damon Hill, David Coulthard, Roger Clark, Colin McRae, Richard Burns, Carlos Sainz, Hannu Mikkola – they've all been here at various times. I remember one particular evening when the legendary Sir Jack Brabham, David Hobbs, Tony Mason and five-time Le Mans winner Derek Bell were all here quite coincidentally, sitting at different tables.

As for the lady drivers – I won't hear a thing said against them! Tony first introduced us to Louise Aitken-Walker, the young Scottish girl who became the Ladies World Rally Champion, and we all fell in love with her. She was fantastic! All of us at The Butcher's Arms felt a special bond of affinity after the 1990 Rally of Portugal during which she and her co-driver thankfully survived one of the most spectacular crashes in rally history. After skidding on a mountain road, their car somersaulted down a ravine and plunged into a deep lake, where Louise was trapped underwater for several heart-stopping seconds before managing to free herself. As all this happened not very far from Vinha, we followed her career with even greater interest from then on.

Later on, Tony also introduced us to sisters Stephanie and Rachael Simmonite, hugely successful both in off-road racing and rallying, together becoming British and French Champions. Photographer Harry Rhodes, another great character and a very old friend of mine, had been commissioned to do some glamorous pictures of them for a national magazine and these were shot on the patio here at The Butcher's Arms, with the girls changing their outfits in the ladies' loo.

Tony Mason has even managed to leave his mark in there! It was he who started bringing the people from Pirelli tyres here for business lunches and they liked it so much that they kept finding excuses to come back, despite the fact that their office was some distance away in Burton-on-Trent. After a while I got to know them very well indeed and eventually talked them into letting me have some special prints from the world famous Pirelli calendar series, which I framed and hung in the gents' loo. These tasteful but very sexy pin-ups caused so much comment that certain lady customers then started demanding some male crumpet for their loo, which I duly organised. This, in turn, excited so much interest that the men then wanted to go in and see what all the fuss was about. It has got to the stage where we now regularly have to get Terri McGregor to organise guided tours, standing guard outside while the men have a look around the ladies' and their wives check out the gents'.

The story of the early years at The Butcher's Arms would not be complete without a mention of two special customers for whom I came to have the greatest admiration and whose friendship I always valued highly – the late John Profumo and Tom Wheatcroft, the owner of Donington Park motor racing circuit.

I think probably everybody respects the enormously dignified way in which John Profumo conducted himself in the aftermath of the scandal that ruined a potentially brilliant political career. He never complained and never tried to explain himself or to make excuses. Instead he quietly and simply dedicated himself without any fuss to the full-time charity work that he was still doing right up until the time of his death in 2006.

He was, without question, one of the most charming people I have ever met. I first got to know him in the days when he and his wife, the former actress Valerie Hobson, used to be among the regulars at The Westgate Arms. I was just the barman, but he treated me then in exactly the same friendly way as he did when I became the proprietor at The Butcher's Arms. At one time, when he and Valerie were still living at Avon Carrow, they used to come here at least once a week and we would always talk gardening, he himself being a keen and very knowledgeable gardener. I was just starting to develop the garden here at the time and he would often walk round with me after lunch or before dinner, giving me lots of useful tips.

Later he and Valerie moved to a village in Hampshire where, together, they created their own beautiful garden. I didn't see so much of them from then on, but the pale yellow Wedding Rose that John created and gave to me in 1975, and which I planted in a prominent spot at the front corner of the building, continues to flourish, a permanent reminder of a very special man.

Compared to the smoothly urbane John Profumo, Tom Wheatcroft is very much a rough diamond. A self-made man, Tom started as little more than freelance labourer, digging foundations under contract before going on to become a multi millionaire construction boss, responsible for building half of Leicester. A great motorsport enthusiast, he used part of his fortune to buy and revive the Donington Park circuit, where he had watched car and motorcycle racing as a boy in the 1930s and where he went on to set up one of the finest vintage car museums in the world.

His great ambition was always to re-establish the circuit as a regular Formula 1 Grand Prix venue, along with Silverstone and Brands Hatch. He devoted many years and invested a great deal of money in trying to fulfil this dream and then, having eventually succeeded in securing the right to stage the 1993 European Grand Prix, had to stand by in helpless frustration as the event got stuck in the mud, torrential rain throughout the weekend turning the place into a quagmire.

However, he has always had the consolation of knowing that the event will forever be remembered for what is generally acknowledged to have been one of the most remarkable drives of the late, great Ayrton Senna's brilliant career. In appalling conditions that had led the experts to predict in advance that overtaking would be almost impossible, Senna went from 5th to 1st in the course of a sensational first lap that is considered by aficionados to have been the most spectacular in all of F1 history. In winning the race, he lapped everybody, including second-placed Damon Hill. Peter, who was there on the day, says that this performance alone made it all worthwhile.

Peter in the gardens outside the Palacio de Seteais during a visit to Portugal, with Augusta and with me alongside the prized Volvo 122s that I acquired from Gerald Gold.

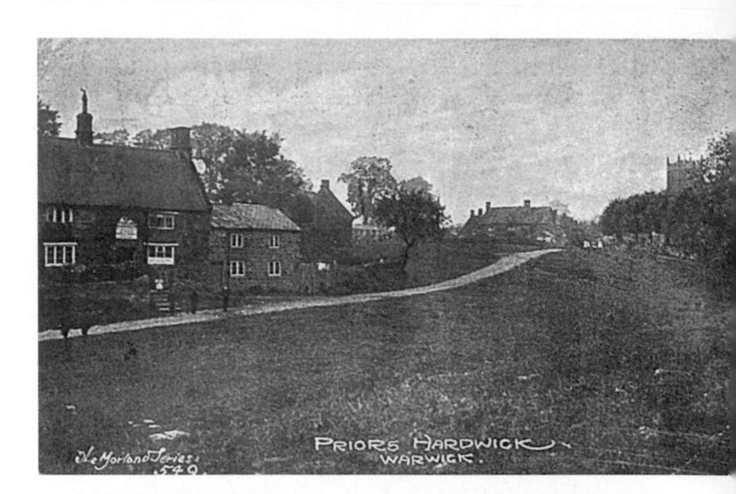

(Right): The Butcher's Arms at the turn of the century and (below) as it was shortly before we took over in 1973.

64

Down Your Way

Feast of life at 'doomed' village

Ross Reyburn meets the Portuguese restaurateur who put a tiny English village back on the map.

FACT FILE

Great publicity in the Birmingham Post *and (facing page) our first ever menu, featuring prices that may well bring a nostalgic tear to many a reader's eye.*

THE BUTCHER'S ARMS
PRIORS HARDWICK
Telephone
Byfield 60504

This old Inn has plenty of history standing as it does in the centre of the Royalist stronghold during the Royalist wars. Cannon balls from these times have been found in the area. Certainly the Inn is older than the Church, which is unusual because it was quite common for an Inn to be built at the same time, so that the workmen could use it for lodging and drinking. Situated just off the old Welsh road, the Inn must have seen many cattle drovers pass with their beasts, on their way to London.

Menu

Priors Hardwick

Telephone Byfield 60504

MENU

STARTERS

Home Made Soup 15p
Egg Mayonnaise 25p
Ravioli 25p
Paté Mason 30p
Prawn Cocktail 30p
Grapefruit Cocktail 20p
Fruit Juices 15p

SPECIALITIES

MAIN COURSES

Fried Scampi 90p
Grilled Halibut 90p
Poached Trout 80p
Fried Fillet of Plaice 80p
Gammon, Egg and Pineapple 85p
Sirloin Steak £1.30p
'T' Bone Steak £1.40p
Grilled Chicken 90p

SWEETS

Home Made Sherry Trifle 20p
Apple Pie 20p
Strawberry Flan 25p
Ice Cream 15p
Chocolate Gateau 30p

Cheese 15p

COFFEE SPECIALITIES

Gaelic Coffee 35p
French Coffee 35p
Jamaican Coffee 35p
Coffee with Whipped Cream 10p

WINE LIST

CHAMPAGNE

No. 1 Chasseur Freres £1.82 £3.65
2 Pol Roger 1964 £2.91 £4.85
3 Lanson Black Label £2.39 £4.80
4 Veuve Clicquot N.V. £2.56 £4.80

SPARKLING WINE

5 Varichon et Clerc Sec *extra dry* £1.28 £2.50
6 Asti Spumante Martini *sweet* £1.04 £2.10

PORTUGUESE

7 Mateus Rose £0.83 £1.60

SPANISH

8 Rose *medium dry* £0.53 £1.20
9 Sauternes *sweet* £0.53 £1.20

BORDEAUX WHITE

10 Barsac, Sichel *rich and full* £0.93 £1.85

BURGUNDY WHITE

11 Chablis Caves Syndicales *dry and light* £0.84 £1.65
12 Meursault 1970, Pierre Ponnelle *full of flavour* £1.28 £2.60
13 Puligny Montrachet 'Les Demoiselles' 1964 (French Bottled) *fine and full bodied* £1.81 £3.60

RHINE

14 Liebfraumilch Blue Nun *medium dry* £1.06 £2.10
15 Crown of Crowns Liebfraumilch *medium dry* £1.02 £2.05
16 Niersteiner Domtal 1970, Jacob Horz (bottled in Germany) *fine and fruity* £0.86 £1.65

MOSELLE

17 Berncasteler Riesling 1970, Jacob Horz (Bottled in Germany) £0.84 £1.65
18 Zeltinger 1970, Jacob Horz (Bottled in Germany) *light and dry* £0.85 £1.70

YUGOSLAVIA

19 Lutomer Riesling *medium flavour* £0.58 £1.20

BURGUNDY RED

20 Beaujolais *young, fresh and fruity* £0.64 £1.30
21 Cotes de Beaune Villages, 1970, Vienot *delicate light body* £1.16 £2.40
22 Nuits St. Georges 1970, Vienot *fine and well balanced* £1.17 £2.40
23 Gevrey Chambertin, Jules Regnier *good sound fruity wine* £1.30 £2.60
24 Vougeot Clos de Prieure 1966, Pierre Ponnelle (French Bottled) *delicious* £2.30 £4.60

CLARET

25 Club Claret, de Luze, *light body, good flavour* £0.63 £1.50
26 Chateau Peconnet, Premieres Cotes de Bordeaux *mature and fruity* £0.79 £1.60
27 Chateau Fonbadet 1969, Pauillac, *fine and full bodied* £0.91 £1.85
28 Chateau Lynch Bages 1967, Pauillac (Chateau Bottled) *excellent* £2.17 £4.20

Reserve du Patron White (dry) £1.90
Red (medium dry) £1.90

Portuguese Red: Litre bottles (Bottled in Portugal) £0.70 £1.50

Tony Mason (far right) and Roger Clark were re-united eighteen years after their 1972 British Rally triumph when they came out of retirement to take part in the 1990 Pirelli Classic Marathon Rally in the MGB with which they are pictured here.

Jaguar's 1988 Le Mans-winning car flanked on the left by (l to r) drivers Jan Lammers, Andy Wallace and Johnny Dumfries (now the Earl of Bute) and on the right by (l to r) Jaguar executives Sir John Egan (Chairman), Roger Putnam (Sales and Marketing Director) and the late David Boole (Public Affairs Director), all Butcher's Arms regulars, and Tom Walkinshaw, who ran the Le Mans racing team for Jaguar.

COOL Kitten

This is the Grandaughter of local restauranteur, Leno Pires who is a keen Jaguar fan owning several superb examples of the marque

(Above): With David Hobbs and the E-type that nearly came back on a low loader and (left) a rather special young lady posing with the same car for the Jaguar staff magazine Topics.

Peter and Helen on their wedding day, with the vintage Bentley that brought them from the church to the reception

The groom's parents in relaxed and happy mood.

John Bowe, his wife Emma and Peter (back row) with (front, l to r) Joanna Lumley, Richard Griffiths, Heather Griffiths, Richard Madeley and Judy Finnegan at John's birthday dinner.

Our lucky birthday boy Michael Mac in action in his showjumping heyday.

(Clockwise from the top): The legendary Sir Jack Brabham, Ian Botham and rally girl Louise Aitken-Walker – just three of the many celebrity customers who have visited The Butcher's Arms over the years.

At the time of writing, Donington is being lined up to take over from Silverstone as the venue for the British Grand Prix. If that plan goes ahead it will give Tom enormous, if rather belated satisfaction.

I think part of the reason that he and I have always got on so well is that, like me, he started out with nothing. When Tom came out of the army after the war he started up a small business that prepared building sites up to ground level, basically digging out the footings and putting in the foundations and the drainage and so on, all of it by hand. He loves to tell the story of how, on his very first contract, he was working with an Irish labourer called Mick, whom he had hired to help him do the digging. He said to Mick: "We'll start from each end of the first trench and when we meet in the middle we'll take a tea break." They set to work and after a couple of hours Mick downed tools and announced: "Right, that's done. I'll have my tea now."

"Hang on," said Tom. "We're supposed to meet in the middle."

"To be sure, but I've finished my half," replied Mick with a grin.

That man worked for Tom for the rest of his life and Tom still has the very spade he used that day. He went to Mick's funeral and was horrified when he saw that the grave, which had been dug with a machine, was not quite straight. "I was so cross," he told me. "That man had been spot-on with everything he did. If I'd known they were going to make such a mess of it I would have gone and dug his grave myself, by hand." And he meant it. Tom Wheatcroft is that sort of man and I am proud to be able call him a friend.

The success of that early period at The Butcher's Arms was clouded for me by the loss of both my parents within three years of each other, my mother dying in particularly upsetting circumstances. My father went first, in 1975, and was buried in the little local cemetery at Sarnadas da Simao. Our two worlds had become very different, of course and although he had visited us at Priors Hardwick and was obviously pleased and proud that I had done so well for myself, I don't think he could really relate to the life I had created for myself in England.

Quite understandably, he found it all a little bewildering and was only too happy to get back to Vinha. When he died it soon became clear that my mother simply couldn't live without him. Her sister, Alexandrina, who was still living next door, got in touch to warn me: "Your mother is pining away, Lino. If you don't come and get her she will not survive long."

I immediately arranged for her to come to Priors Hardwick. She lived in the house next door, where I did my best to make her feel at home by trying to create the same sort of environment that she was used to, even going so far as to make a vegetable patch in the garden where she could continue to grow her own vegetables, just as she had always done back in Vinha. A little old peasant lady, dressed from head to foot in black and looking strangely incongruous in a Warwickshire village, she would get up at five o'clock every morning, as she always had done, and would then slave away all day in her garden – working to forget, I suppose.

Then one terrible day we found her dead, drowned in a pond in the garden, and it turned out that she had taken her own life. It is an episode that I still find it difficult to talk about even now. Only those who have lost someone close to them in the same distressing circumstances will perhaps be able to understand not just the grief that I felt but also the hurt. It was as if everything that I'd achieved in my life and all that I'd tried to do for her over the years counted for nothing. In the end, it seemed, she didn't really care for me at all, only for my father. How, otherwise, could she have done what she did? I don't think I will ever be able to come to terms with that.

We arranged to have her body taken back to Portugal where she lies buried, next to my father, in the hillside cemetery at Sarnadas. It is a pretty spot and when I stand at the graveside the memories and the emotions come flooding back to me. Above all there is the poignant recognition, as I look out over the wooded valley, that while my parents will always belong there, I no longer do.

JOKERS, JAGS AND GERANIUMS

Imagine for a moment that you have just taken delivery of the classic E-type Jaguar that you had always dreamed of owning. It is your pride and joy, the sort of car to be taken out on special days, and, even then, only when the weather is fine, with no risk of getting mud spattered on the gleaming white paintwork. However, when a couple of old friends, who also happen to be classic car freaks themselves, then pop in to admire your new toy, get behind the wheel and start playing with the controls, what more natural than that you should invite them to take it for a quick spin? Fantastic! No problem! But what if they should be away a little longer than you expected and that when they eventually return the car to you an hour or so later it arrives on the back of a low loader? How would you feel then!

Tony Mason and photographer Harry Rhodes – 'Harry the Flasher' as he delights in introducing himself, pausing a moment for dramatic effect before explaining that this is a reference to flash photography – could picture the full horror of my likely reaction in their mind's eye. And, being wicked practical jokers, it was temptation beyond endurance when they happened to spot an RAC breakdown truck parked in a lay-by as they were putting the car through its paces on the Southam by-pass.

They immediately pulled over and asked the driver if he would collude with them in a little harmless deception. Would he, for a few bob, quickly load up the E-type and deliver it round the corner to The Butcher's Arms? Fortunately for the state of my nerves, the driver was a bit of a 'Jobsworth' – "More than my job's worth to do that, mate" – so their little plan came to nothing, much to Harry's huge disappointment. "I would have given anything just to see the look on your face, Lino," he sighed, rubbing his hands gleefully and giggling at the prospect like a naughty schoolboy.

That E-type was one in a long line of Jaguars and Daimlers that Peter and I have owned between us over the years. My special relationship with the company itself, signified by the Jaguar lapel pin worn by me and all my staff, dates right back to my days at The Westgate Arms when I used to serve Sir William Lyons, the founder himself. Sir William went on to become a regular at The Butcher's Arms, as did 'Lofty' England, followed from then on by a succession of chairmen and top executives, including Sir John Egan, John Morgan, Bill Hayden, Roger Putnam and Nick Scheele. All of them used the restaurant privately as well as for business lunches and various corporate events, becoming not only highly valued customers but also great personal friends.

I like to think that I was sometimes as good for their business as they were for mine. Former Export Sales Director John Morgan, in particular, seemed to find me especially useful when it came to wining and dining his more important foreign clients. An impressively patrician figure, silver-haired, softly spoken and always immaculately dressed in a beautifully cut, pinstripe suit, John is every inch the perfect English gentleman.

Now retired, he was also an outstanding businessman, a gifted linguist and a great ambassador, not just for Jaguar but for British industry as a whole. It was his great misfortune, however, to find himself in the hot seat during that difficult period under British Leyland in the seventies when Jaguars briefly became notoriously unreliable. There were times when John needed all his powers of diplomacy to pacify angry VIP customers and he would quite often enlist my help in this respect. "I'm bringing in someone really difficult today, Lino," he would warn me in advance. "Do me a favour and make sure he gets the full treatment."

I remember one particularly delicate situation that he had to deal with that arose from the sale of a fleet of twenty Daimlers to an Arab sheikh. Special air conditioning had been requested to cope with the desert heat but Jaguar had rather overdone it and the systems that were fitted were so fierce that the ladies of the harem would emerge at the end of a journey looking totally dishevelled, hair blown all over the place, as if they had just come in out of a Force Ten gale.

The unhappy sheikh sent the entire consignment back in disgust and John was left to smooth things over with the dealer who had arranged the sale. He had signalled a red alert when he made the booking for lunch and as soon as they arrived I duly launched into a major charm offensive. By the time they time they got to the coffee and liqueurs the dealer was all smiles again and John, looking mightily relieved, added a handsome tip to the bill. I am happy to say that I have been able to provide a similar sort of service for many more of my regular business customers and I think it would be fair to say that, partly as a result, some very important deals have been finalised over lunch here.

In that respect we may even have played our own small part in the Ford takeover that ensured Jaguar's survival after the dark days under British Leyland, when the Brown's Lane headquarters of one of the most illustrious marques in British motoring history became known simply as 'Large Car Assembly Plant No 2'. Sir John Egan, who successfully masterminded the vital takeover, certainly used the restaurant a great deal for business lunches and, as a memento of his many visits, presented me with a special mounted Jaguar motif inscribed 'To Lino Pires – The Perfect Host'.

His successors, Bill Hayden and then Nick Scheele also became regulars, with Nick and his wife Ros even arranging for their son's wedding reception to be held here in the restaurant. Nick, the man credited with restoring Jaguar to its former glory after the Ford takeover, also had his official Farewell Dinner with us before moving over to the parent company in 1999 and again in 2001 when he went on to even greater things as No 2 at Ford in America.

Roger Putnam, who followed John Morgan as Director of World Sales and Marketing before he also moved over to Ford as UK Chairman in 2002, kept up the Butcher's Arms tradition. Roger first came here with John when they were lunching a Japanese contact

– John included a working knowledge of Japanese among his many linguistic skills – and I didn't see him again until we happened to bump into each other at Heathrow Airport almost a year later. He was running the Jaguar Racing Programme at the time and was bound for the Nürburgring while I was on my way to Portugal when we both found ourselves marooned in the departure lounge, our flights delayed by fog.

I recognised him immediately, which quite impressed Roger when I went up and re-introduced myself. As we started chatting, we then found that we had quite a lot in common. His in-laws had lived in Portugal for many years and the local Jaguar agent in Lisbon was a good friend of his. "Do you happen to know him?" he asked. "Very well," I replied with a smile. "In fact, he is meeting me at the airport with my E-type."

From then on we became, to quote the phrase I like to use on such occasions, Friends Forever. Roger has been a regular at The Butcher's Arms ever since and, one way and another during that time, I have managed to return the compliment by indirectly putting quite a bit of business his way. He once said to me: "Lino, I don't know whether my secretary is working for me or you – she seems to spend most of her time arranging test drives for your VIP contacts."

He added, however, that as the test drives almost invariably ended in a sale, he wasn't about to complain. His successor, Jonathan Browning, when asked why the restaurant was so popular with Jaguar executives, duly listed the quality of the food, the wine and the service before adding with a smile: "Apart from that, Lino seems to be the best salesman in the company – and we don't even have to pay him!"

I was sometimes able to surprise even people involved themselves in the motor industry with the level of my contacts at Brown's Lane. When Jill Sutton was trying to buy the new S Type as a special 60th birthday present for her husband she couldn't get the particular colour spec and trim she wanted for love or money because of the long waiting list. When I heard that she had given up trying to get it in time for the big day I made a couple of phone calls and managed to get the car delivered within twenty-four hours.

The S-type was the last Jaguar to be styled by the late Geoff Lawson, the design genius who was also responsible for the XK8, the XJ8 and the fantastically beautiful but also, as it turned out, rather too fabulously expensive XJ220. Greatly missed by everyone following his sudden and untimely death, Geoff and his wife, Jill, lived just down the road from us at Napton and were long-time Butcher's Arms regulars, as is another brilliant young stylist, Gerry McGovern. With his bushy-haired rock star looks and his stunning girlfriends, Gerry, best known for his MGF design, cuts an unmistakably glamorous figure whenever he's in the dining room.

It is not just the high-flying executives at Jaguar with whom I am proud to have built a special relationship. Among the prized mementoes that you will find dotted around the restaurant is a large wooden key, cut from the burr walnut veneer used in the fascias of all top-of-the-range Jaguar models and inscribed with the message 'The Key To Success Is Individuality'. This was presented to me by one of the craftsmen who make the fascias by hand and who had actually made the one in my own particular car. I met him during a tour of the factory and was so impressed by his craftsmanship that I invited him and his wife over for dinner. It was when he then returned some time later as a paying customer that he presented me with the key. He had even found a section of veneer with a knot in it that resembled a jaguar's head.

I came by my first Jaguar rather unexpectedly after a smooth-talking businessman, whose company had an account with The Butcher's Arms, persuaded me to buy his Daimler from him. I was reluctant at first, explaining to him that if my customers saw me driving such a splendid car they might think I was making too much money, but this chap was a real salesman.

"Look at it this way, Lino," he suggested. "If I was in Banbury with some important friends and I saw you getting out of a Daimler,

I wouldn't hesitate to introduce you to my friends, who would probably be very impressed and might then decide to try your restaurant. On the other hand, if I saw you getting out of a scruffy car, I probably wouldn't even bother to introduce you."

This all seemed to make pretty good sense so I went ahead and bought the car from him. Not long afterwards, however, I was rather alarmed to hear that he had gone missing, along with £30,000 from his company's accounts! Not wanting to take the slightest risk of being associated with anything underhand – especially as he had asked me to pay him in cash! – I took the car straight to the Jaguar dealer in Leamington and traded it in for a brand new Daimler Double Six.

This was in 1978, by which time we were so well established and doing such good business that I felt I could safely afford such an extravagance. At around the same time, I also bought what was then a tiny two-room cottage next door to The Butcher's Arms. The original idea was that Augusta and I would live there ourselves, instead of being 'over the shop', but although we did it up and extended it to a very high standard over the next few years, even putting in an indoor swimming pool, we never actually moved in. We found, in the end, that it was actually more convenient to be able to pop upstairs rather than have to go out and walk thirty or forty yards down the road all the time, so we only ever really used it as a guesthouse for friends and family.

The other great attraction of the property when we originally bought it was that it came with several acres of land, adjoining what we already had behind the restaurant. This enabled Augusta and I to set about creating the garden that was to spread out rapidly over the next few years from what is now the patio to form one of the most famous features of The Butcher's Arms, a showpiece that eventually became the subject of a Gardeners' World television programme.

Given the fact that in our younger days back in Portugal we had both hated having to work on our family farms, it might seem strange that we should take on a project that involved a huge amount of equally back-breaking toil at a time when we were already more than busy enough with the restaurant. Maybe, it had something to do with our peasant genes revealing themselves! Perhaps, subconsciously, we yearned to get back to our roots.

The main reason was actually that we needed a spare time interest that would provide us both with a regular and easily accessible escape from the crushing seven-days-a-week routine of running the business. Gardening was the obvious answer. It was something that I had started to get into when we were working for the Tahany family at Claybrooke Grange, where part of my job involved looking after the garden. Augusta and I had then developed a liking for formal gardens, occasionally driving out on our free Sunday afternoons and evenings in the summer to visit places like Hidcote and Kifsgate. This was what inspired us with the idea of doing something similar at The Butcher's Arms.

Obviously, it couldn't be anywhere near as grand as some of the classic English country gardens we admired so much, but we were nevertheless determined to make sure that it was a bit special and with this in mind, we started looking around for someone to help us design and landscape a basic layout. We didn't have to look very far because living just down the road in Priors Marston was a remarkable lady called Valery Stevenson.

Born in Salzburg, Valery had trained as a gardener from the age of sixteen. After qualifying at a horticultural college in Germany, where she specialised in garden design, she got a job with a municipal gardens department. Here, during the war years, she suddenly found herself, at twenty-five, in charge of five hundred gardening staff. Their responsibilities included not just all the parks, gardens and cemeteries but also some extensive nursery and vegetable gardens.

When the war ended and the allied occupying forces moved in, the commanding officer of the local British Army unit inquired as to whether she might be able to supply his men with fresh vegetables on a regular basis. Valery said that she would be happy to do so if, in return, he could possibly find a job on the base for her nephew. This was duly agreed and it was through the nephew that she met another British officer who shared her interest in art and who was brought by the nephew to see some of the paintings that were hanging in the house where she was living at the time. They fell in love and married and, in 1948, returned together to England where her husband got a job as a librarian in Warwick. Shortly after that they moved into the cottage in Priors Marston.

Valery decided to set up as a freelance garden designer and, although she had a thin time of it during the years of immediate post-war austerity, she eventually became very successful and went on to design more than three hundred large gardens, mostly in the Midlands but also as far away as York. The plans that she drew up for us were fantastic, as meticulous and as detailed as any architectural drawings. The bare meadow plot we presented her with was ideal in the way that it was on a South-facing slope but a bit awkward insofar as the slope was rather too steep. Very cleverly, Valery designed the shape of the beds and placed trees, shrubs and flowers of varying heights in such a way as to give the optical effect of reducing the gradient.

No sooner were her plans and planting schedules ready than Augusta and I set to work with a vengeance. In what was to become a regular daily routine for the next few years, especially through the spring, summer and early autumn months, I would be up at dawn every morning, often getting started in the garden at 5.00 or 6.00am and putting in four or five hours before coming in and sprucing myself up in readiness to greet the early arrivals for lunch.

Augusta, who was busy in the kitchen first thing in the mornings, would get out to join me in the afternoons. While I did most of the heavy spadework, she would get on with the weeding and pruning and, together, we did all the planting. Literally thousands of trees, shrubs and flowers went into that garden, including more than fifty different varieties of rose alone, and I can honestly say that, between us, Augusta and I planted every single one in the entire four-and-a-half acres.

Doing everything ourselves, rather than hiring a full-time gardener, involved a tremendous amount of hard work but it was worth it in every way. As Valery Stevenson has always said, you never get quite the same pleasure from a garden if you are not the gardener yourself. Mind you, that was probably not quite true of the amorous couple who, in full view of a packed terrace, got so carried away over lunch one summer afternoon that they eventually took themselves off into the bushes for the sort of dessert that was definitely not on the menu! But, in general, Valery is absolutely right. If you buy a house with a ready-made garden you never love it quite as much as you do when it is something you have created yourself out of nothing.

Valery had helped us to choose a selection of plants that would ensure there was always something in flower at every time of year, with a riot of colour throughout the summer. As well as massed begonias, pansies, peonies, delphiniums, azaleas, roses of every kind and all the usual cottage garden favourites, there were exotic tropical plants in huge terracotta pots, rare ornamental fruit trees and all manner of highly-scented flowering shrubs.

The focal point was a large lake, complete with waterfall and spanned by a rustic bridge from which you could watch huge koi carp gliding under tiger lily pads. I had always wanted a water feature and in order to create the lake I bought what was not much more than a ditch, running along the bottom boundary of our property, along with a bit of land immediately on the far side that would be flooded once I had dammed the stream to form the lake. When I called my solicitor to arrange the conveyancing he looked at me as if I was mad. "Lino," he said, shaking his head, "you are the only person I have ever come across who would want to buy a ditch." Later, when he saw the lake in all its glory, he understood.

We are on clay in Priors Hardwick, which meant that the ground was hard to work with at first and needed to be broken down with plenty of manure. As it happened, the great World Champion show jumper Caroline Bradley and her family lived at Priors Marston at the time and were regular customers and so I said to her: "Caroline, I need a lot of manure for my garden – could you possibly let me have some from your stable?"

She very kindly said that I could have as much as I wanted and soon afterwards started sending me hundreds of plastic bags filled with the stuff. Fantastic! I covered the whole garden with it and felt very pleased with myself until, come the spring, weeds suddenly sprouted everywhere, even in places where there had been none before. It was a bloody nightmare!

"Oh dear, Lino," said Caroline when I told her what had happened. "Didn't you know? You have to let the stuff rot down for at least a couple of winters before you put it on the land in order to make sure all the weed seeds have been killed off."

Poor Caroline. She was such a lovely girl and it came as the most terrible shock to all of us when, not long after this, she collapsed and died suddenly from a heart attack while actually taking part in an event. She was only in her early thirties. I knew all her family very well – her mother still comes in occasionally – and they were, of course, totally shattered by this awful tragedy, as was everyone who knew her. That she died doing what she loved most was no real consolation.

We lost another very dear friend in similarly circumstances when farmer and amateur National Hunt jockey John Thorne died while riding in a point-to-point just up the road at Mollington. I had first got to know John well at The Westgate. He was a colourful character, with a great sense of humour, and whenever he booked in you always knew it would be a lively evening. His twin daughters both followed him into the saddle, one going on to become the first woman ever to ride in the Grand National – but only after John had famously taken the Jockey Club to court to overturn the men-only rule.

The girls still come in and Mrs Thorne actually presented me with the whip that John was using on the day that he died. She told me: "I know he would have liked you to have it because he thought the world of you." That was a very proud moment for me because I felt exactly the same about him, a very special man in all sorts of ways.

The regular customers all took an interest in watching our garden grow, none more so than John Profumo. A keen gardener himself, Jack was always giving me useful little tips, including the idea of using a length of hosepipe laid out on the ground to help you decide the best shape for a new flowerbed. Fellow Tories Lord Heseltine and Lord Lawson were also among those who would make a special point of taking a turn around the lake whenever they were here. Lord Heseltine, in particular, was extremely knowledgeable about the trees and shrubs we were planting and was kind enough to invite me to visit his arboretum at Thenford.

He would often bring the whole family here for Sunday lunch and as they are all great dog lovers, Roger, our resident Alsatian at the time, would be given a special dispensation to come into the dining room whenever they were here, just so that the children could say hello to him. Roger, who was not normally allowed in, got to know this and would start getting excited the moment they arrived in the car park.

I only occasionally talked politics with Michael, but I firmly believe that the Tory party made a terrible mistake when they rejected him as leader. At that particular time they desperately needed a man with his kind of charisma and by turning their back on him they succeeded only in shooting themselves in the foot. He seemed to me to be, almost literally, head and shoulders above any other candidate. And from a selfish point of view, it would have been nice to be able to boast that we had a Prime Minister among our regular customers!

Lord Lawson also used to come here with his family when he was living in the area. This was after his time at No 11 but before he went on the famous diet that reduced him to a mere shadow of his former self and which was so startlingly effective that he went on to write a book about it. He and his wife, Therese, have since moved away and now spend much of their time in France so we haven't seen them for some time. Even if they were still living in this part of the world, I don't think he would be able to indulge in too many Butcher's Arms' lunches if he wanted to maintain the new, slimmed-down figure that left him looking almost unrecognisable.

I sympathise with him in that respect because following a health scare back in 1989, I, too, have had to watch my diet very carefully. Often I will have no more than an orange for breakfast, a cup of soup at lunchtime, a couple of pieces of toast and honey and a cup of chocolate at around 5 o'clock – and that will be it for the day. Once or twice a week I may have something a bit more substantial for lunch, some fish or chicken possibly, but Sunday is the only day when I allow myself a full meal and a good bottle of wine.

My favourite dish, if I'm going to spoil myself, is Steak Diane. The recipe we use here is the one that came down from the Savoy to The Three Horse Shoes with Jack Spencer in 1954 and from there, via The Westgate, to us. I do love my food and it takes a massive effort of willpower for me to eat so sparingly, so I can well imagine just how difficult it must have been for Lord Lawson.

Having got to know him quite well, I was able to do him a small favour when he was looking for housekeeping staff, arranging for a Portuguese couple to go and work for him. He turned out to be a very generous employer and provided them with a number of rather nice perks, including a Rover car. This, however, led to an amusing comedy of errors when the couple flew home to Portugal for a holiday and asked me if I could organise for John Austin, who works for Peter and who also doubles as an occasional chauffeur, to drive them up to the airport in the Rover.

They spoke very little English so there wasn't a lot of conversation on the way up to Heathrow, but when they got there John decided he'd better just pop into the terminal building to make sure they knew where to go, leaving the car parked at the drop-off zone. He was only away for a few minutes but, needless to say, by the time he got back the car had already been towed away. Things then got even more complicated when he went to reclaim it. You can imagine roughly how the ensuing conversation went.

"Could you just confirm the registration number, Sir?"

"I'm afraid I can't remember it – the car doesn't actually belong to me."

"O.K. So, who is the owner?"

"I'm afraid I can't tell you that either. It belongs to this Portuguese couple that I've just dropped off. They don't speak any English and I only know them by their first names."

"Hmm. I see, Sir. Well, if you'll just wait there a minute while we check the computer... ."

The police computer duly revealed, of course, that the car was registered in Lord Lawson's name and suddenly John found himself with quite a bit of explaining to do. In the end it took a call to Lord Lawson himself to convince them that John hadn't actually nicked it.

As the business went from strength to strength and the restaurant gradually advanced ever further across the patio, Peter was fast growing up behind the scenes. Shortly after we took over at The Butcher's Arms he had started boarding at Emscote Lawn in Warwick. Augusta was in tears about that at first, of course, but our evening routine in the restaurant made it impossible for him to continue as a day pupil because it meant deserting him from about six o'clock onwards and leaving him to get on with his homework alone before putting himself to bed. We did try it for a short while but it was not satisfactory and very soon, after coming upstairs once or twice in the middle of the evening to find him asleep on the floor in front of the television, even Augusta agreed that it made sense for him to become a weekly boarder.

His career at Emscote was fairly uneventful but ended on a high note when he won a place at Rugby. Headmaster Jonathan Riley was reluctant to put him in for the entrance exam, convinced that he had no hope of passing, but I insisted. Ever since I had been shown around the school all those years before it had been my great ambition to send a son of mine there one day. "I have this dream," I said to Mr Riley. "So, please, put him down for the exam." To my great delight, Peter passed with flying colours.

One of the proudest moments of my life was when I drove him there and dropped him off with his trunk and his tuck box on the first day of term. I couldn't help thinking back to that day when I had gone with my mother to beg for a place in the little school at Paiágua. And I found myself wondering what the Professora would have said if someone had told her then that this little peasant boy would one day be sending his son to one of the most famous schools in the world? On this occasion it was not only Augusta who had a tear in her eye and a lump in her throat.

While by no means the stuff of Tom Brown's Schooldays, Rugby, in the seventies, was still very much an old-fashioned public school, with large, cold, high-ceilinged dorms, iron bedsteads and strict discipline. Even so, Peter loved his time there and made many great friends, including Simon Saunders, who was to be Best Man at his wedding. The only blip on his school record was when he got sent home for a week after being caught drinking. Instead of exploding, I am the type who goes silent when angry and I think our drive home when I went to pick him up that time was the only journey we have endured without a word being spoken.

On the other hand, one of the highlights of his Rugby career was the metalwork project for which, at the age of sixteen, he completely rebuilt a Lancia Fulvia sports car. Partly because of the many car industry and motor racing people who were regulars at the restaurant, Peter was already car mad by this time. He and his mate Jim Cross, whose family then owned the large farmhouse behind us where Peter himself now lives, used to buy up old MOT failures from the local scrap dealer for £30-£40, tinker about with them and drive them around the fields belonging to the farm until they finally gave up the ghost, whereupon the scrap dealer would come and take them away again.

Augusta's nephew Eric, who was still working for us at this time, had a Lancia Fulvia, which was quite a sexy little 2+2 Italian sports car with a 1300cc engine, and when Peter spotted an advert in *Exchange & Mart* for one that had burnt out after an engine fire he decided to buy it and do it up as his school project. It took him six months altogether and not only did he get top marks for his effort, but the car served him well for several years. He took his test in it and to celebrate the passing of their A levels he and his other great friend, Greg Hobbs, later took it all the way to Portugal and back for a holiday, stopping off on the way down to visit Peter's cousin in the South of France. They did the return journey from Paiágua to Priors Hardwick – a distance of nearly 1500 miles – in less than 24 hours! And this despite losing nearly two hours on the last lap due to overheating problems in the engine that caused the fuel to vaporise and forced them to keep stopping at regular intervals in order to let it cool down. He thought it wiser, at the time, not to reveal the full hair-raising details of the trip to his mother.

As everybody who ever drove with her will be well aware, Augusta was always a very nervous passenger, especially when I was behind the wheel! She herself was the proud owner of a sporty white Porsche 928S but drove it very sedately – and without ever apparently engaging reverse gear! She would spend a lot of time searching for parking spaces that she could go into forwards. Clearly unaware of this was the gentleman who left a note on the windscreen one day while she was having her hair done in Leamington. He was very impressed, he wrote, to see such an attractive woman of her age driving such an amazing car. "I would love you to take me for a spin in it," he added in a rather spidery scrawl. "If you fancy going for a drink some time just give me a call." And, signing himself simply 'Sam', he left a number. Augusta, who resisted the temptation to ring the number and find out more about her secret admirer, was never allowed to forget this.

Meanwhile, I was busy urging Peter to start thinking seriously about his future. It had always been my hope that he would follow me into the business and one day take it over. So, long before he finally made up his mind that this was indeed what he wanted to do, I had taken the precaution of putting his name down for the world's top catering college, the Ecole Hoteliere de Lausanne in Switzerland. The place is a bit like Eton insofar as you have to get your name down early to stand a chance of being accepted. Peter did toy for a while with the idea of reading either Law or Economics at university and, with his love of cars, even thought about opening a garage or car dealership. In the end, however, he decided that the restaurant business offered him a more certain future and duly took up his place at Lausanne in 1983.

We had gone down together in advance to have a look around the place. When John Morgan at Jaguar heard about the projected trip and learned that I was planning to fly to Geneva and drive down from there he told me: "Don't hire a car – I'll organise transport for you." And when we arrived in Zurich, there waiting for us was a brand new XJS, with just 300 miles on the clock. It was ours for the whole week that we were there, but with thick snow everywhere I didn't really get to make the most of it, driving very sedately for fear of getting into a skid and putting a dent in it.

Peter, once he had started at the college, was much less inhibited in the Golf GTI that had by then replaced the Lancia, regularly racing home to Priors Hardwick whenever he had a few days off. On one or two occasions, most notably for Greg Hobbs' 21st, he drove back just for the weekend. With music blaring from the 16-speaker sound system, he would leave Lausanne after his last lecture on a Friday afternoon, arrive home in the early hours of Saturday morning, spend Saturday and Sunday partying and then set off on the 12-hour trip back to Switzerland on Sunday evening, arriving just in time for the breakfast shift on Monday morning.

Given such a hectic schedule, it is perhaps not really surprising that he didn't last the full course.

FAST FOODIES

At 9.00 pm one busy Saturday night, with the restaurant already packed to capacity, a coach pulled up outside and disgorged a party of thirty-six people, all of them clearly looking forward to a good dinner after a long day out at the Royal Show. Unfortunately, their arrival had come as a completely unexpected surprise. It emerged later that they had indeed phoned to make the reservation some days beforehand, but whoever had taken the call had simply forgotten to put it in the book.

This was the awkward situation that Peter faced on the very first occasion that he was left in charge of the restaurant on his own, Augusta and I having gone off to Portugal together for a short holiday. Talk about being thrown in at the deep end! Overbooking on such a scale is any restaurateur's worst nightmare. Peter, however, handled the crisis very calmly, plying everybody with free drinks and nibbles and somehow managing to keep them happy for over an hour until tables became available. I couldn't have done it better myself, a masterpiece of improvisation. I was very impressed when I heard about it and told him so in no uncertain terms, which was the least I could do seeing as I was the one who had taken the reservation in the first place and who had then failed to note it down!

Peter joined the family firm in 1984, a little earlier than anticipated, having dropped out of catering college after just one year of the four-year course. He had found it hard going in Lausanne, mainly because of the fact that the course was conducted entirely in French. Had he been intending to forge an independent career for himself in hotel or restaurant management it would have been worth persevering, because a formal qualification from Lausanne would have guaranteed him a job anywhere in the world. However, having decided that his long-term future lay at The Butcher's Arms he quickly came to the conclusion that he could find out all he needed to know about service, administration and management from the first-hand experience of working alongside Augusta and I. At the same time, as he was quick to point out, he would be saving me an awful lot of money in fees.

I had to agree that this made a lot of sense. And, of course, I was delighted that he wanted to become part of the business. I insisted, however, that he had to start right at the bottom, working behind the bar and then as a waiter with no preferential treatment, no extra Saturday nights off and not the slightest hint in any way that he was getting an easy ride just because he was the boss's son.

Although he has done his fair share of washing up in the kitchen, the only thing he never really tried his hand at was cooking. He knows how to do it – that was the one section of the course at Lausanne that he completed before he left – but, like me, he was never particularly interested in slaving over a hot stove. He always says that he is simply not dextrous enough and not confident enough to work well in that pressurised kitchen environment.

It can often be difficult for a father and son to live and work together as closely as Peter and I have done over the years without eventually getting on each other's nerves and falling out and yet, right from the start, we've always had a fantastic relationship. We get on so well that we will still quite regularly go off on holiday together, just the two of us. And although we might not see eye-to-eye on everything in the office we usually find a way around it without an argument. Part of the secret is that, as time has gone on, we have come to complement each other perfectly within the business and never get in each other's way, Peter being more than happy to concentrate in those areas where I'm not so strong. Basically, that means anything to do with paperwork.

When Augusta and I started off, back in 1973, we muddled through with a little help from a lady in the village who came in on a part-time basis to do the books. It was all relatively simple in those days because the operation was that much smaller and we had only a few suppliers to deal with. But now that we are catering for up to 1,000 customers a week, with a greatly extended menu and a full wine list, we have many more suppliers making daily deliveries. Keeping track of that is a full-time job in itself. Peter now takes care of all the ordering and buying as well as most of the general administration, leaving me free to get on with looking after everything front-of-house.

As for my overall business sense, I was very flattered and extremely surprised to hear that leading businessman and management consultant John Sadiq, one of our most regular customers during the many years when he was living just down the road in Lower Boddington, uses me as a model when he is preaching the fundamentals of good business practice to his clients in his capacity as a sought-after 'company doctor'. John apparently lists good marketing, a clear understanding of customers' requirements, employee satisfaction, the consistent quality and presentation of the product and after-sales follow-through as the key points. But he puts his finger on it when he goes on to say that I seem to achieve all of this without actually being aware that I'm doing it! That's absolutely right. I don't go in for any detailed analysis, forward projections or anything like that. I just keep a check on my bank statements each month and look at the balance sheet at the end of the year and as long as the percentage profit is about the same, I'm happy.

Peter, in many ways, is much more organised and businesslike than I am. I have always tended to rely more on energy, enthusiasm and what Peter refers to with a certain amount of exasperation as sheer blind faith. Let's face it, that's what brought me to England in the first place and what prompted me to buy The Butcher's Arms, unseen, from a man I met in a bar at two o'clock in the morning. I am impulsive and intuitive and most of the time it seems to work pretty well – although not always, I have to admit.

In 1985, purely out of curiosity, I popped into a local auction in Stockton on my way over to collect some strawberries from the local Pick-Your-Own fruit farm and emerged a few minutes later as the owner of The Crown public house. I certainly hadn't gone there with any real intention of buying the place, but as nobody seemed willing to open the bidding I thought it would be a good idea just to start the ball rolling. Unfortunately it didn't roll any further and the auctioneer knocked it down to me at that price.

It was all very embarrassing because I didn't even have my chequebook with me. All I had in my pocket was a single cheque with which to pay the owner of the P-Y-O, which I had to make out to the auctioneer instead. I'm not sure that fruit farmer Leslie Williamson entirely believed me when I explained that I would have to pay him later because I'd used his cheque to buy a pub on the way over!

I had a lot more explaining to do when I got back to Augusta, but somehow managed to convince her that it was a shrewd business move. The Crown was actually a very nice little pub, especially once we had done it up. As manager, I installed Mary Nicholls, the very attractive 22-year-old daughter of a great farmer friend and neighbour in Priors Hardwick.

Described in the local newspaper that covered the grand re-opening as a 'Bet Lynch lookalike', Mary was a lovely, bubbly young blonde who did a great job of pulling in the customers but who wasn't quite so hot on the business side, with the result that we never actually made much money. Unfortunately, I simply didn't have the time to give The Crown the personal attention it needed so, after a couple of years, I sold it to a Portuguese couple I knew who were looking for a place of their own, having previously worked for me for a while.

The Craven Arms at Southam, which I bought from the brewery as an investment, was another venture that didn't work out quite as well as I had hoped. First, the sitting tenant to whom I was leasing it went bankrupt, owing me a large amount of money. Then, when a Birmingham property developer made me a very handsome offer for the site, I turned him down because I had grand plans of my own to build a little shopping centre there. That never happened for various reasons and I realised, too late, that I had missed the boat. From this experience I learned the very valuable lesson that you should never be too greedy, that you should always be content to let somebody else have a bit of the cream once you've had a chance to take a decent profit for yourself. That has been my philosophy ever since.

In the end I did all right out of the Craven Arms, selling the car park separately as the site for a small housing development. There was also a rather strange and quite unexpected bonus when I discovered later that I also owned the public urinal next door! This only emerged when the council decided to build a new one elsewhere in the town. It turned out that the old one stood on land that had been leased from the Craven Arms many years before. I sold it for quite a tidy sum to the same builder who had bought the car park and he put up another house on the site, although he turned down our suggestion of naming it West Craven (WC for short)!

Back at Priors Hardwick there was certainly more than enough to keep me fully occupied. With the economy taking off again in the eighties under Maggie Thatcher, business was booming as never before. You can take the economic pulse of a nation in its restaurants and the rude health of UK plc at that time was evident in our packed dining rooms. Eating out had never been more widely fashionable.

It was at around this time that David and Jill Sutton moved into the area, David having just relocated his motorsport business from London to Daventry. A leading figure on the World Rally scene for more than twenty years, he made his name as a rally team manager with victories in the British Championship in 1980 – with a Ford driven by Ari Vatanen and David Richards – followed by the World Championship the next year before going on to record seventeen wins with Audi. After that, he concentrated on preparing rally cars for wealthy amateur individuals as well as for works teams and also set up a wonderful classic rally car museum, Historic Motorsport.

When he and Jill moved into their first home in the area, the previous owners kindly left them a list of useful contacts – the local milkman, newsagent, garage, doctor and so on. It also included local places to eat, with The Butcher's Arms right at the top of the list. David, however, got a bit of a shock on his first visit.

Having enjoyed a fairly expensive meal, it was only when he came to pay the bill that he discovered we didn't accept any credit cards, only cash or personal cheques. He was not by any means the first person to get caught unawares by this deliberate house policy at the time, but we always made sure it didn't cause any embarrassment. We would simply say to people: "Don't worry, you don't have to pay now. Just take the bill with you and put a cheque in the post." I had worked out that credit card commissions would cost me upwards of £20,000-a-year and I reckoned that on that basis we could afford to have quite a few people take advantage of the system by abusing our trust and failing to pay up and yet still be quids in.

In fact, most people were so impressed by the way in which we allowed them to walk out without any fuss, not even asking for an address, that, just as David did on this occasion, they would mostly fall over themselves to get their cheques to us as quickly as possible. I can only remember one person who failed to pay up in the end.

The system was actually quite a positive marketing ploy, bringing us what almost amounted to a cult following thanks to incredulous customers from as far away as America and Australia going away and telling their friends about this extraordinary restaurant where, even as complete strangers, they had been allowed to walk out without paying on the casual understanding that they would send a cheque when they got home. I especially remember a Jaguar dealer from California who brought some people to lunch here and ran up a bill of over £300 that he was allowed to take back to America with him. He never got over it and, partly as a result, makes a point of coming back every time he's in the country, never failing to regale his guests with the story.

It was only relatively recently that we eventually had to give in and start taking credit cards, simply because their use had become so widespread that it was no longer practical to refuse them. With more and more big business clients needing to charge their entertaining expenses through a corporate credit card it became a problem and an issue so, very reluctantly, we had to fall in with everybody else. It cost me a fortune in commission and I don't think the move brought in any new customers.

With a business such as ours that has been built up on a word-of-mouth reputation, I don't think that being in the restaurant guides helps that much either. We were featured in the Good Food Guide for some years before suddenly being dropped for no apparent reason, but our trade didn't suffer at all as a result. The only thing that upset me was a niggling suspicion about the circumstances leading to our expulsion.

It followed a rare incident where a difficult couple were so rude and unpleasant to the staff that I had to ask then to leave. As usual in such situations, I didn't charge them but made it plain that they would not be welcome again. As they left, the man snarled at me that he had connections and that he would make sure I was kicked out of the Good Food Guide. I don't know for sure that our subsequent omission was down to him but it is irritating to think that it might have been, given his appalling behaviour.

Fortunately, we have had very few really awkward customers over the years. The only other example that I can recall involved a party of three people who complained that their Chateaubriand wasn't the genuine article. Interestingly, the matter was only raised after they'd eaten every last mouthful. The complaint was ridiculous and my immediate suspicion was that they were simply trying it on, hoping to get out of paying. So, when they persisted in kicking up a major fuss, I used a ploy that I had learned from Jack Spencer, simply removing their table to leave them sitting in splendid isolation in the middle of the restaurant, looking conspicuously silly. They soon took the hint. Once again, I told them that I didn't want their money or their custom in future and that was the last we saw of them.

David Sutton, meanwhile, was not at all put off by the experience of falling foul of our credit card policy and he and Jill have been regulars ever since, bringing with them a whole lot more celebrity customers from the world of motorsport, including the great Hannu Mikkola. Hannu had just won the World Rally Championship for Audi when David first brought him in, a visit that provided a vintage moment of embarrassment for Peter.

Peter had only just started working here and although he was heavily into motorsport he had failed to recognise Hannu. Realising this, David asked casually what Peter thought of the Audi Quattro and Peter, rising to the bait, replied that, as it happened, he had just driven one and didn't think that much of it. He then proceeded to go into his reasons in some detail. David let him finish and then, with a big grin on his face, introduced Hannu, one of the greatest Rally drivers of all time, who had just won the World Championship - in a Quattro!

Through people like David Sutton, Andrew Cowan, David Richards and Tony Mason I have got to know almost everybody who is anybody in the rallying world over the years, to the extent that when David Sutton and Jill very kindly invited me to the Portuguese Rally as their guests not so long ago I found myself getting a big welcome in almost every garage in the entire service area, despite the tight security that normally means you can't go anywhere without a whole array of special passes.

At the same time, the proximity of Silverstone has ensured that we also get a steady stream of people from Formula 1, especially around the time of the British Grand Prix. Things have changed in Formula 1 even in the time that we have been in business so that you don't often get the drivers themselves in here over the race weekend any more. The sport is so competitive these days that they have to live like monks most of the time, existing on strict diets and exercise routines dreamed up by full-time health and fitness therapists. Tony Mason did bring the brilliant young Toyota driver Allan McNish here recently and all he wanted for lunch was a little bit of fish and a glass of milk, which, of course, we duly produced.

Things tended to be a lot more relaxed in the heyday of characters like John Watson and Derek Bell. One of Derek's more recent visits here was as the guest celebrity at a special dealer promotion for the new Audi S8. As part of the programme he was taking people out for a spin in the car and obviously putting it through its not inconsiderable paces around the local country lanes. One or two of the dealers came back looking a little green about the gills but Derek waited until it was turn of the Audi PR people before really pulling all the stops out. When they reeled out of the car afterwards they were goggle-eyed and open-mouthed, with legs turned to jelly, while Derek's face was wreathed in mischievous smiles.

Among the Formula 1 crowd who started using the Butcher's Arms regularly in the eighties, two of my favourites were Paul Morgan and Mario Ilien, founders of Ilmor Engineering, the Northamptonshire-based racing engine specialists who have famously designed and built race-winning engines for Indycars in America and then, since 1994, for McLaren.

Always looking for any excuse to celebrate, Paul and Mario held their very first Ilmor office party here. Their main backer, the legendary American businessman, entrepreneur and race team owner Roger Penske, flew over from the States and, as always when Paul and Mario were around, it was a very lively affair. We had a nebuchadnezzar of champagne on display in the restaurant at the time and, jokingly, they asked if it was for them. "Not until you win your first Championship," I replied. They were back the next year, having done just that, to claim the giant, 20-bottle nebuchadnezzar.

Ilmor engines totally dominated Indycar racing for several years after that and Paul and Mario then moved into Formula 1, enjoying an almost equally successful run there with McLaren. Before long, the little company that they had started in the kitchen of Paul's farmhouse home was so big that they had to hire major venues for their annual office bashes, places big enough to accommodate a staff that had grown to over three hundred. Meanwhile, both Paul and Mario continued to come to The Butcher's Arms with their wives, Liz and Catherine.

Tragically, Paul was then killed in a flying accident in 2001 when the vintage World War II aircraft that he used to fly as a hobby crashed as he was coming in to land at Northampton's Sywell airport, not far from the Ilmor base at Brixworth. With his colourful, fun-loving personality, he was a man who both worked hard and played hard and he is sadly missed by all of us who knew him well and whose lives he helped to brighten up.

Of all the great motor racing figures, past and present, who have visited The Butcher's Arms over the years the one who I was perhaps most thrilled to see here was Sir Stirling Moss. He had always been one of my great heroes from the real daredevil days of motor racing. I asked him if he would let me have a signed photograph for the wall and he said with a smile: "Certainly – but it will cost you another bottle of that excellent Portuguese wine we've been drinking." As he left, I slipped a case of it into the boot of his car.

Stirling was one of many celebrities from all walks of life who have been brought here by Tony Mason. As a presenter for TV's Top Gear and also a writer for various motoring magazines, Tony was regularly meeting and interviewing all sorts of interesting people and he would always try to work it so that he could do the interview over lunch at The Butcher's Arms. In the run-up to the 1994 RAC Rally we converted a back room at the restaurant into a television studio so that he could conduct interviews over dinner with the three Subaru drivers, Colin McRae, Richard Burns and Carlos Sainz.

One star he unfortunately didn't quite manage to bring here, though not for lack of trying, was comedian Ken Dodd. Tony, who had once fancied himself as a bit of a stand-up comedian, had met "the squire of Knotty Ash" by chance through his television work and had subsequently got to know him very well. He was a great fan anyway and would regularly go to see his shows, usually popping round to the dressing room afterwards for a drink. On one occasion he even took the glamorous rallying Simmonite sisters along with him, which, of course, went down very well.

He has got a fund of priceless stories about Ken, including one about the time when he offered to use his contacts in the motor industry to get Ken a new Jaguar at a very handsome discount. Ken, of course, has a reputation for being a bit careful with his money. "By Jove, that would be fantastic," he told Tony, adding: "If you can arrange that I'll get you a free video of my new Christmas Special TV show." Tony was never quite sure whether or not that was meant to be a joke.

As part of a Guinness Book of Records attempt, Ken is trying to appear in every single theatre and cabaret club in the country, however small, and when Tony heard that he was booked into the working men's club in nearby Woodford Halse he decided it was a perfect opportunity to get him along to The Butcher's Arms, either for lunch beforehand or dinner afterwards.

The problem was that Ken apparently likes to drive himself home to Knotty Ash after every show, no matter where he happens to be appearing, and he then sleeps in late the next morning before setting off for the next evening's engagement. That meant he couldn't get down in time for lunch. Tony therefore arranged for me to stay open late so that they could come over together after the show.

Well aware that Ken's shows famously tend to go on and on for hours, he reckoned that they could still make it by about 11pm. Unfortunately, however, Ken got lost on the way down, went on late and didn't finally come off stage until well after midnight, by which time he just wanted to get straight on the road back to Knotty

Ash. So, much to our disappointment, we never did discover just how tickled we might have been, missus!

Among the many showbiz personalities we *have* been able to welcome here, and whose pictures line the walls, are fellow comedians Bobby Davro and Jasper Carrott. Also, a rather unlikely character known as Tony 'Banger' Walsh. Tony acquired his nickname during a twenty-year professional wrestling career during which he regularly tangled with the likes of Giant Haystacks and Big Daddy. Having retired from the ring to become a 'minder', he then formed a very successful security company called Mayfair Security Services that has provided personal protection for every top celebrity from Madonna to Michael Jackson, from George Michael to Robbie Williams and from Phil Collins to Paul McCartney.

At the same time Tony became an actor himself, appearing in many film and television roles. And for good measure he has also written a screenplay and a very entertaining autobiography. A gentle man, despite his heavyweight professional background, he usually comes in with his family and is nearly always here on special occasions such as Christmas Eve and Mothering Sunday. When he and Peter found that they were going to be in Dubai at the same time they arranged to meet for lunch at the seven-star Burj Al Arab restaurant, only to find as they sat down that another Butcher's Arms regular, Leicester businessman John Thomas, was sitting at the next table. It's a small world – or maybe it's just that Butcher's Arms customers go to all the best places!

Local TV presenter Kay Alexander and actor John Bowe both held their wedding receptions at The Butcher's Arms. John Bowe, who starred as the serial killer in the original Prime Suspect, is the most charming man in real life, while his wife, Emma Harbour, whose family live in Nether Heyford and whose father is the actor Michael Harbour, has been coming to The Butcher's Arms since she was a child.

John told me that their first date had been at The Butcher's Arms. They were filming part of the TV series 'Trainer' together near Redditch, he explained, and when he asked Emma if she knew anywhere special in the area where they could go for dinner she immediately thought of us. "It was a magical summer evening, with the sun and the moon in the sky at the same time," he remembers. "And we actually had our first kiss on the conversation chair in your entrance hall."

The wedding itself took place in the village church, after which everybody walked down the road to the restaurant. Best Man was 'Pie In The Sky' star Richard Griffiths, who gave a hilarious speech. And among the star-studded guest list were Helen Worth – Gail Tilsley in 'Coronation Street' – and the Absolutely Fabulous Joanna Lumley. Did I manage to give Joanna my usual welcoming kiss? You bet!

Equally glamorous, Selina Scott was at the peak of her popularity when she came here to shoot some publicity pictures connected with the launch of a new Peugeot car. Selina had a reputation in the Press at the time for being rather distant and difficult but we found her to be exactly the opposite. I remember it being a freezing cold day and yet she was required to wear very light clothing for the photo session, which took place outside in the car park. The poor girl was turning blue as the photographer shot roll after roll of film in his efforts to get exactly the picture he wanted and yet she never made the slightest fuss. As you can imagine, there were plenty of gallant male admirers volunteering to help her keep warm in between shots, me included!

With business going so well and with Peter there to hold the fort in our absence, Augusta and I were at last free to take more time off together, enjoying regular breaks back in Portugal where, by now, we had a villa. We had started looking for a holiday home there in the late seventies and in 1978 came very close to buying a property just outside Sintra from actress Gloria Swanson. I never actually got to meet the great star, but we spoke several times on the phone and I still have a letter from her in which she talks about her "little oasis". In fact, it was a large six-bedroom house, complete with a separate studio and servants' quarters. The setting, in an acre of garden and with an orchard overlooking the Atlantic, was very attractive, but with negotiations already well under way a search unfortunately revealed that there were plans to open a caravan camping site right next to it so we changed our minds.

The first house we bought was not far away in the same very pleasant residential area, but that turned out to be too close to a rather noisy road so we sold it and then found a perfect plot of land just a bit further along the coast at Colares. Just four miles from the Palacio de Seteais, it is in a beautiful, unspoilt location looking down on Praia Grande, regarded as one of the best beaches in Portugal. It was actually on that very beach that Augusta and I once used to spend our afternoons off all those years ago when we were working in Sintra, travelling the short distance from the town centre on the old tram that still runs along part of the route. Here we built our own villa, facing almost due west with stunning views towards the setting sun.

We later bought and sold several plots along the same stretch of coast, including one on which the Minister of Health has built a large, modern-style villa and another which is rumoured to have been bought by an even more important Government figure. These days, the poor boy from Vinha has got some pretty illustrious neighbours!

When it comes to investment, I'm only really interested in land or property. I've never had any stocks and shares and there's no point in leaving your money in the bank or building society. I am also proud to say that I have never had to take a penny out of the UK to fund my property investments in Portugal. Everything I have there now was originally funded purely out of the land in Vinha and Paiágua that Augusta and I inherited from our families and later sold.

Our timing was perfect. Twenty-five years ago, people who had left our villages and had done well for themselves were going back and buying up land there, partly just to show off. For a while these

Two views of the garden we created on the land behind the restaurant and (below) the TV crew led by Stefan Buczacki who filmed it for Gardeners' World.

Me with Apollo astronaut Colonel Tom Stafford and his wife Linda (on the right of the picture) along with Mr and Mrs Andrew Barr. Andrew, a former Rover Group director, got to know Tom through business contacts in America.

'Banjo Bob' Norton showing his musical versatility while his guitar gently weeps!

With Augusta at our villa in Portugal (top), taking aim while on holiday in South Africa with Derek Salt (above left) and Augusta with Tim and Judith Pearson in Florida.

Men behaving stupidly – me with Andrew Guest at Henley Regatta.

Augusta and me with Helen and Peter and grandchildren Heather and Edward outside The Butcher's Arms (right) and the whole family on holiday at Cascais after Peter had been given the all-clear following successful cancer treatment at the Royal Marsden.

Me, Peter, Helen and the grandchildren with the replica Ferrari that I bought as a birthday present for Edward.

(Left): Getting the chequered flag from Tony Mason and (below) Professor David Cunningham receiving a cheque from Peter after the Ferrari had been raffled, raising £40,000 for the Royal Marsden Hospital.

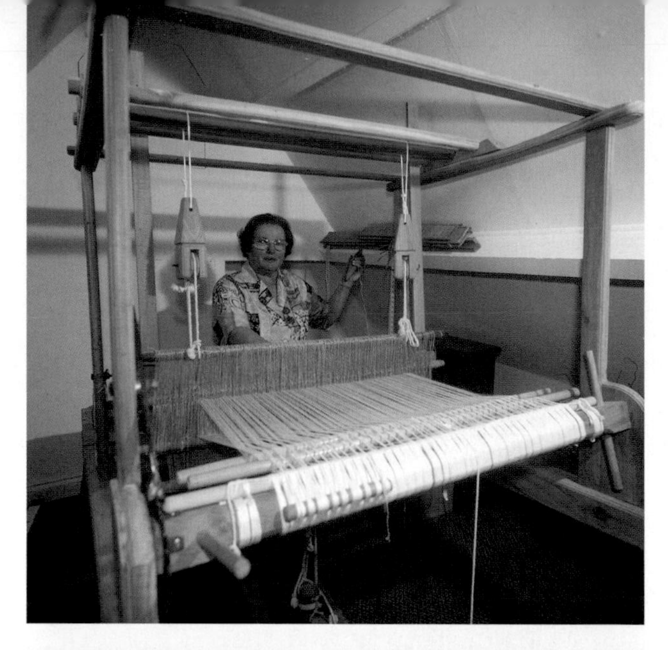

Augusta upstairs at The Butcher's Arms, working on the loom made for her by Antonio Dias, the village craftsman from Paiágua. Antonio had never been out of Portugal until he came over to Priors Hardwick to assemble the loom.

Right):With writer Mike Cable, doing essential research for the book in the cellars of my Portuguese wine supplier Paulo da Silva at Azenhas do Mar.

(Below): With Augusta and the staff at The Butcher's Arms in 2002. Seated next to me at the front is long-serving 'Trolley Dolly' Terri McGregor. Current restaurant manager Nuno Correia is on the far right next to his predecessor, Steve Syvret.

Proud moments with Portuguese President Jorge Sampaio (right) and Ambassador Antonio Gregorio (Left) at the London Guildhall and (below) with John Major at a Gala Evening in memory of Lord Prentice of Daventry, the former Conservative Minister.

Speaking at Augusta's funeral (clockwise from the top): Baroness Knight, David Hobbs, Peter Tahany, Sue Moore and granddaughter Heather.

people were covering the place in pound notes, but I guessed that in the long-term it would be worth very little. On the coast was where you needed to be, because that was where all the development was going to come. And, of course, I was right. Today, the house in which I grew up and the land that went with it is worth virtually nothing whereas, up in Colares, I am sitting on a goldmine.

As it happens, it's a goldmine that did actually originate with two solid gold bars. I say that because when I first started selling some of my parents' land in Vinha, the Portuguese economy was rather unsettled so I decided that the safest thing to do would be to buy gold with the proceeds until such time as we wanted to invest in a new property. We bought the two 1kg ingots from a jeweller, which was perfectly legal at that time, and kept them hidden under a clay pot at my father's house. When he died, we moved them to my sister-in-law's house in Paiágua but she then started to worry about having the responsibility so, the next time we were over there, Peter and I took it to the bank in Castelo Branco with the aim of keeping it there in a safety deposit box.

This led to a scene, very funny in retrospect but not quite so amusing at the time, in which we found ourselves standing in a long queue, each with a very heavy gold bar stuffed into a coat pocket. After shuffling slowly forward for what seemed like an age we eventually got to the counter, only to be told that we would first have to get the gold registered with a solicitor and complete all sorts of other formalities before we could actually make the deposit. As we were due to leave later that day for England we simply didn't have the time so we had to take it straight round to the jeweller and sell it for cash.

My timing on this occasion time was not so good because shortly afterwards the price of gold shot up from £30-an-ounce to nearly £100-an-ounce. Nevertheless, it was that money, plus what we later got from selling some of the land that Augusta had inherited from her family, that eventually enabled us to buy our first property in Sintra.

In almost every respect the eighties had proved to be a golden decade as far as we were concerned and it closed on a high note on August 19th, 1989 with Peter's marriage to Helen. The two of them had met for the first time five years earlier when Peter and some of his friends gate-crashed Helen's 18th birthday party in the village hall at Staverton, where her family then lived. A few days later they bumped into each other again, not entirely by chance, and Peter invited her to join him at a friend's 21st, a rather grand affair held at Hambleton Hall. Things just went from there and she became his first and only serious girlfriend.

Like Peter himself, Augusta and I soon fell in love with Helen. Stunningly attractive, she also has great strength of personality, a quality that has shone through in the most testing circumstances in recent years. No parent could hope for a better daughter-in-law. In fact, I look upon her now not as my daughter-in-law but simply as my daughter.

The wedding took place in the local Roman Catholic church in Southam, followed by a reception at The Butcher's Arms, the first time in the sixteen years that we had been there that we had ever been closed all day. The newlyweds were chauffeured from the church to the reception in a vintage 1930s, 8-litre Bentley driven by its owner Reg Parker, a regular customer for many years and an old family friend, now sadly no longer with us.

A wealthy garage owner from Nuneaton, Reg used to come with his wife to The Butcher's Arms for lunch every Sunday without fail throughout the summer, always arriving in fine style at the wheel of one of the Bentleys, Ferraris or Aston Martins from his fabulous collection of classic cars. When he heard that Peter and Helen were getting married he invited them to go and have a look at the collection, telling them: "Choose any one you want and I will gladly drive it for you on your wedding day".

Peter chose the Le Mans Bentley, which Helen was not too thrilled about on the day as her hair got blown all over the place in the back of the open car. Then, to cap it all, they got stuck behind a tractor pulling a trailer full of manure on the narrow country lane leading into the village, eventually making a less than totally dignified entrance in front of the assembled guests. Everybody had a good laugh about that but Helen had no need to worry – she looked absolutely fantastic. Augusta, of course, was in tears – but for once they were tears of happiness rather than anxiety.

Earlier in the week, Best Man Simon Saunders, a friend since his Rugby days, had arranged to take Peter to dinner at Le Manoir Aux Quat' Saisons and this was followed by slightly more raucous stag night celebration at Alexio's, the Greek restaurant in Chipping Camden, where a belly dancer provided the traditional embarrassment for the bridegroom.

Twenty-five members of our family came over from Portugal for the wedding and to keep them entertained during their extended stay I hired a minibus to take them round to all the local tourist attractions. There were contingents of Helen's family from both Dublin and Birmingham and also close friends from among our ever-expanding Butcher's Arms community. One way and another, a pretty good party mix! As we drank our toasts and waved the happy couple off on their honeymoon I had every reason to feel very pleased with life. The next decade, however was to bring one or two nasty shocks.

ALARMS AND EXCURSIONS

At around eleven o'clock one evening at the end of 1989 I was upstairs, relaxing with a cup of coffee at the end of another busy night in the restaurant, when I was suddenly hit by what seemed like a severe attack of cramp. Staggering to my feet, I managed to take a few steps around the room until the pain gradually eased. My first reaction was to put it down to the fact that I had been doing rather a lot of heavy digging in the garden that afternoon. Maybe I had overdone it a bit, I thought to myself. However, when the same thing happened again the next morning I decided I had better go and see my GP, Peter Middleton, and almost before I knew what was happening I found myself in the John Radcliffe having extensive tests.

These revealed that I had been uncomfortably close to a major heart attack and had probably got away with it only because I was so fit as a result of all the exercise I was getting in the garden. What was now urgently required, I was told, was either a by-pass operation or the recently developed angioplasty treatment that involved widening the arteries by passing a microscopic bulb through them.

In the circumstances there seemed no point in delaying things so I told them to get on with whatever needed be done as quickly as possible and arrangements were made to admit me straightaway, with a view to carrying out the operation the following day. This came as a bit of a shock to everybody at Priors Hardwick when I phoned them with the news since they thought I had just gone in for a fairly routine check-up.

By early the next morning I was being wheeled into theatre. Although an angioplasty involves a slightly riskier procedure than a by-pass, the overall benefits of avoiding major surgery are considerable and the consultant had decided that because I was so strong I would be a suitable case for this new, state-of-the-art treatment. I later discovered that I was one of the first people in Oxford to have it.

The first face I saw when I came round afterwards was that of the young Australian medical technician who was in charge of checking all the monitoring equipment. I was vaguely aware that the surgeon and his team were discussing my case on the other side of the screen but I couldn't quite hear what was being said. I whispered to the technician: "What are they saying? Did it go all right?" He said: "I'm afraid I'm not allowed to tell you anything, you'll have to wait for the consultant." But I persisted. "If you can't say anything, just give me a sign," I said. And, at that, he grinned and stuck both thumbs up.

That one little gesture gave me such a lot of confidence. I immediately warmed to him and wanted to show my appreciation. Having discovered that his girlfriend was a nurse on the ward and that her birthday was coming up in a few weeks' time, I told him that I would very much like to invite the two of them to dinner at my house. I didn't mention that I owned a restaurant. On the night, I sent a taxi to pick them up and bring them over to The Butcher's Arms where we gave them an evening to remember, complete with a birthday cake. It being a Saturday, the place was packed and I made a point of telling everybody how this cheerful young Aussie had been responsible for giving me a wonderful boost just when I most needed it.

In the end I was in hospital for only three days and despite being put on permanent medication and warned to watch my diet a bit more carefully in future, I soon felt fit as a fiddle again and very quickly got back into the old routine.

The restaurant was so well established by now that the economic downturn of the late eighties and early nineties barely affected us. If anything we were busier than ever thanks partly to the introduction of set menu lunches. At a very reasonable fixed price and with no hidden extras, this proved enormously popular with older customers who took full advantage of the opportunity to eat in a quality environment without having to break the bank. At the same time, the garden provided a great, added attraction throughout the summer months, especially once it had been featured on BBC TV's Gardeners' World in 1990.

Once again, this had come about through Tony Mason. Tony always says that his television career began at The Butcher's Arms because it was here, over lunch, that he successfully 'auditioned' for the job as a presenter on Top Gear that got him started. He had been approached by the programme producer, Dennis Adams, who asked if he could recommend a mutually convenient restaurant where they could meet for lunch, preferably somewhere nice but out of the way. Tony immediately suggested that they come here.

Anxious to make sure that everything went particularly well he then briefed me in advance about what was going on so that I could do my bit to help and, without going over the top, I proceeded to give them my best VIP treatment. I don't know how much difference it all made, but Tony duly got the job.

A couple of years later Dennis Adams was put in charge of all programmes being made at Pebble Mill under the heading of Leisure, including Gardeners' World. Tony happened to be chatting to him one day shortly after that and reminded him of the great lunch they'd had here, pointing out that there was a fantastic garden attached to the restaurant that might make a really good item for the programme, especially as a pub garden had never been featured before. He then brought him here for lunch again, so that he could do a recce. When I showed him around the garden, he was suitably impressed and immediately gave the go-ahead.

Presenter Stefan Buczacki and the team spent a whole day filming the half-hour programme. It was a great thrill for Augusta and me to see our creation up on screen and to have a professional praising our amateur efforts so generously. We explained that it was a joint effort, although I had to admit that when it came to clearing out or severely pruning shrubs and bushes that had become untidy I sometimes made arbitrary decisions that could only be carried out when Augusta was not around, since she tended to become very protective about certain plants and wouldn't let me touch them. I would have to wait until she made her regular Friday visit to the hairdresser or went over to the villa in Portugal on her own for a few days and by the time she came back the damage would have been done! Usually she would accept that it was for the best but got so cross with me on some occasions that she wouldn't speak to me for several days.

The weekend after the programme was transmitted the car park outside was jammed as never before with people wanting to have a look round. They had come from all over the country and from then on we started having regular Open Days. In the first year we raised over £4,000 for charity by charging just £1-a-head to non-diners.

Eventually, however, we found that the responsibility of looking after the garden and maintaining it as a showpiece was becoming a bit too much for us. By now it involved a huge amount of work all year round and simply to keep it under control at the height of the season meant I would often be out there at dawn, having not got to bed until midnight the night before after working in the restaurant all evening. And with so many people now wanting to walk around it all the time, we found that we were no longer able to get out there whenever we felt like it to work in a relaxed way without being disturbed. What had once been a pleasure was starting to become a chore. On top of all that, Peter and Helen had started a family and Augusta and I wanted to be able to spend more of our spare time with the grandchildren. Reluctantly, we decided that the garden would have to go.

We finally sold it in 1995, together with the house next door. This had become something of a white elephant, remaining unoccupied for much of the time, except when we had guests staying. Peter and Helen, who had been living in a small two-bedroom cottage in the village that they had bought and done up shortly after getting married, were urgently looking for somewhere bigger now that the children had started arriving, but the place wasn't really suitable for them. Apart from the fact that they would have found the garden equally difficult to look after, they were understandably worried about having the children running around with the lake there. They had their eye, instead, on Manor Farm, conveniently located immediately behind The Butcher's Arms, which had come up for sale.

Peter knew this house well, having been best friends for many years with Jim Cross, the son of a previous owner. Another advantage, as far as Peter was concerned, was that it had since become rather dilapidated and was ripe for complete renovation, which meant that he and Helen would be able to stamp it with their own personal style. Coming with forty acres of farmland that could be profitably leased out, it had all the makings of an ideal family home, just two minutes walk from the restaurant. So, having received a very good offer for the place next door, we effectively did a swap.

All three of Peter and Helen's children were born in the month of May which, as his friends take mischievous delight in reminding him, seems to reflect the fact that, with a job that keeps him busy six nights-a-week, the only time he gets to see Helen is when he is on holiday in August! In each case, Peter was present at the birth, starting with Heather in 1991 and followed at two-year intervals by Edward and James. With the last two, in particular, everything went so smoothly that Edward was able to go home for tea, having been born at lunchtime, while James arrived just before breakfast and was at Priors Hardwick with mum in time for lunch. Heather took a little bit longer. Peter remembers distinctly that she was born on a Thursday because that's the day that Exchange & Mart comes out each week and he recalls passing the time by as he waited for things to start happening by reading through the classic car adverts! That sounds fairly typical.

Few children can ever have had such doting grandparents. They each have their own very distinct personalities. Heather has always been as bright as a button and very grown-up for her age. Even as a child she liked to write poetry, regularly celebrating family events in verse and invariably bringing a tear to Augusta's eye. The poem she wrote after being taken back to Paiágua to see where Augusta and I grew up is quite remarkable, coming from someone who was just ten at the time, a vivid evocation of our early years there.

She had set her heart on going to Rugby, just like her dad, and although she was taken to see all sorts of top girls' schools, her mind was already made up. We were thrilled when the letter arrived announcing that she had been accepted, one of just twelve successful candidates selected from more than fifty applicants. At the same time, none of us was really surprised. Heather, who has now gone on to University, is a very determined young lady. Clearly she has inherited a few of those ambitious Pires genes!

Edward is a bit like me, I think, very boisterous, very naughty and very good-looking!! One amusing little story sums him up. John Morgan, a friend of ours who runs his own business as a freelance chauffeur, had gone to Heathrow to pick up a family on their return from a holiday in Barbados. Everybody was asleep during the journey down from the airport except the eight-year-old daughter, who was sitting in front, chatting away to John as he drove. She started telling him all about her school, Warwick Preparatory School, and about the boyfriend she had there. "What's his name?" asked John. "Edward Pires," she replied. "I see," said John with a smile. "And why do you like him so much?" "Because he's the naughtiest boy in the school!" came the instant reply. Just like his granddad used to be, I thought, remembering back to my own childhood and those running battles with the boys of Paiágua.

James, the youngest, is like a little miniature version of his dad. I remember him looking through an old family photo album when he was still quite small and coming across a photo of Peter at a birthday party when he was about the same age as James was at the time. As soon as he saw it he said: "Look, that's me – but who are those other boys?" Like Heather, James has followed in Peter's footsteps to Rugby, where he is in the same Kilbracken House that his father was in.

The grandchildren brought a whole new dimension to our lives and this has been echoed in the restaurant, where we regularly find ourselves welcoming the children, grandchildren and even, in a few cases, the great-grandchildren of our original customers. David Hobbs, for example, first came here with his father. David, in turn, then brought his sons Greg and Guy and Greg now comes with his two kids, Andrew and Austin, Andrew being Peter's godson. So, we can proudly claim to be serving the fourth generation of that particular family.

We have high chairs readily available in the restaurant and it has always been my policy to welcome children of any age, even back in the days when this still tended to frowned upon in this country, before exposure to continental holidays opened British eyes to the special delights of dining out en famille. Come in here for Sunday lunch and you will often see almost as many kids as adults, including babes in arms. I love that happy family atmosphere and all the babble and chatter that goes with it. What's more, it makes good business sense. Those children are the adult customers of tomorrow. Catch 'em young, that's what I say!

I think the same relaxed attitude also helps to explain the very special relationship we have with so many of our customers. I like to think of it as my own little club, that huge extended network of people for whom the place is almost like a second home. On a good night, when there happen to be a lot them here together, it's more like a house party than a restaurant and we've had some marvellous moments here over the years.

Regulars are used to seeing the lights dimmed and a cake, complete with candles, being piped in for some unsuspecting birthday boy or girl. It's not often, though, that they get to enjoy the spectacle of a husband being presented with a cake by his extremely attractive wife and a girlfriend, both of them dressed only in the skimpiest of lacy underwear, including stockings and suspenders! The lucky man on this occasion was Michael Mac, the former professional showjumper who famously set a new British record for the high wall in the Puissance at Olympia. Thanks to the lovely Emma Mac and her equally delightful friend, Michael is unlikely ever to forget his 30th birthday. The rest of us who were there that night certainly won't!

Michael has been involved in one or two wild nights at The Butcher's Arms over the years, more often than not in the company of his friend and fellow showjumper Ted Edgar. Nothing could stop those two from enjoying themselves once they'd got the bit between their teeth!

On one occasion, when we were effectively cut off by deep snow, they were towed into the car park by a tractor, Ted's new pick-up having got stuck in a drift on the way over. Along with Ted's sister, Liz, they were the only customers who made it here that night. Upon leaving, they were hardly out of the car park before again becoming stuck and Michael was ordered to get out and push. When the vehicle eventually lurched forward he just about managed to clamber into the back as Ted drove on, not wanting to lose momentum and refusing to stop until they got all the way home, a distance of about three miles. As Michael hung on for grim death, turning blue in the sub-zero temperature, Ted simply roared with laughter, thinking it was all highly amusing.

Not quite so appealing as the vision of a scantily-clad Emma and her friend scampering through the restaurant was the sight of Coventry businessman and long-time friend Roy Meakins making a spectacular Saturday night entrance minus his trousers. Roy had accidentally sat on an after dinner mint, becoming aware of this only when the chocolate melted and a warm, sticky sensation started to spread in the nether regions. After quietly slipping out to the gents to investigate the cause of the problem he then called me into the deserted bar to ask if I could help him to clean up the mess. As I knelt in front of him, inspecting the full extent of the damage at close quarters, another customer emerged from the gents, did a quick double take and, noting my rather startled expression, said with a huge grin on his face: "Please don't let me disturb you, gentlemen!"

At this point I suggested that Roy should take his trousers off so that I could go and sponge them down in the kitchen. I then got distracted by something else and after five minutes or so skulking in a corner of the bar in his shirt tails, Roy, always game for a laugh thought: "To hell with this!" and, still without his trousers, marched boldly back to his table through the packed restaurant. A moment's stunned silence gave way to loud cheers and a round of applause as Roy took a bow.

An incident that went largely unnoticed at the time but which caused great hilarity when related afterwards involved Ted Saunders. As a regular customer and a good friend, especially generous with invitations to his box at Wembley for the Cup Final, Ted knew all about my habit of giving lady customers a welcoming kiss so, arriving at the restaurant one evening with a party that included an American lady whom I had not met before, he executed a nifty manoeuvre to surprise me in a most unexpected manner.

I happened to walk forward to greet his attractive guest just as she was coming up the narrow steps into the restaurant, followed by Ted and his wife, and, as I leant forward to deliver the usual peck on the cheeks, Ted somehow managed to reach round from behind her to goose me without my noticing that it was him. Well, of course, for a moment I thought it was my lucky night! According to Ted, the look on my face was absolutely priceless as I tried to work out whether this demure, innocently smiling lady in front of me had actually been responsible for such a very intimate gesture of friendship!

There was nothing surreptitious about the manner in which a well-known lady horse dealer 'sized up' our waiters one night.

The lady concerned, a colourful character renowned throughout Warwickshire for her earthy, uproarious and totally uninhibited manner, had enjoyed a very good dinner in company with a party that included her two daughters when, at the end of a high-spirited evening, she decided that she was going to find out who, among the waiters, was the most handsomely endowed!

Looking slightly apprehensive, they were duly lined up in the dining room and subjected to the sort of inside leg measurement that could easily bring a tear to the eye, although none of them seemed to mind too much! Amid much mirth, a winner was then declared. And before you start to wonder, let me say that this particular stallion is no longer with us, having moved on some time ago to a new job

On a lively evening you can never be quite sure what you're going to get in the way of spontaneous after-dinner cabaret. When millionaire builder Richard Hayward burst into song with a selection from his favourite musical 'Oklahoma' he so impressed his friend Michael Rosenberg that Michael invited him on the spot to come and sing at his 50th birthday party – in Florida! "You supply the air tickets and I'll be there," joked Richard. In characteristic fashion, Michael not only supplied Concorde tickets to Washington for Richard and his wife but also laid on a private jet to take them down to Florida. And when Richard got up to sing, it was to piano accompaniment supplied by none other than Frank Sinatra's former pianist!

Again on a musical note, the presence in our car park of a Ferrari with the distinctive Channel Islands registration 808, carefully arranged to spell out BOB, is a sign that you could be in for a treat before the evening is out since it means that 'Banjo Bob' Norton is in the house and Bob, brother-in-law of former racing driver Derek Bell, needs no second invitation to fetch a ukulele from the back of the car and run through his impressive repertoire of George Formby classics.

Bob has been a devoted Formby fan ever since his childhood

days in the fifties when his family had a house on the Norfolk Broads next door to the legendary music hall star. Messing around on a water scooter one day, Bob accidentally ran into the back of George's motor cruiser and, having been fished out of the water by George himself, was rewarded with two tickets for the Lancashire comedian's Great Yarmouth show.

A wealthy property developer, Bob now owns the world's largest collection of Formby memorabilia, including his Norton motorcycle and five of his ukuleles, one of which he acquired from the late Beatle George Harrison, a fellow Formby fan. Having mastered the distinctive Formby playing style, Bob can give brilliantly authentic-sounding renderings of all his best-known songs, including When I'm Cleaning Windows, Chinese Laundry Blues and Leaning On A Lamp Post. He's even been featured on television.

A larger-than-life character, Bob was also involved in a famous episode in the restaurant in which a gullible American tourist, who turned out to be the Sheriff of Albuquerque, was taken for a bit of a ride. The Sheriff and his wife happened to find themselves sitting on the next table to Bob and his equally colourful friend 'Knicker Joe' Robinson, so called because he had a hugely successful business manufacturing and supplying underwear to various chain stores around the world.

As I sometimes do with my most regular customers, I took over a complimentary bottle of champagne, jokingly referring to Bob as "My Lord." Noticing that the American couple had pricked up their ears at this, Bob and Joe proceeded to wind them up mercilessly, talking very loudly in exaggeratedly upper class accents and making references to a busy day in 'the House' and their plans to relax with for a spot of falconry. In the end, the Americans couldn't resist the temptation to lean across and introduce themselves. Before long they were convinced that Bob was Lord Guernsey and that Joe was his estate manager, that Magna Carta had been signed at The Butcher's Arms and that most of our game was supplied by His Lordship's falconers. As he left, the Sheriff actually bowed!

Another great character among our regular customers is my old friend Harry 'The Flasher' Rhodes. A bit of a ladies' man, Harry has been married and divorced three times and you could never be quite sure who would be on his arm when he turned up for lunch or dinner. "Don't worry, Harry, it's our little secret," I would whisper discreetly as I led him and yet another new companion to table 14A, the secluded table for two better known to the staff as The Love Nest.

All members of the staff are well versed in the art of discretion. That's essential in a business where you often find yourself dealing with customers who don't seem to know the meaning of the word. You would be amazed how often a man will come in for lunch with his girlfriend, only to re-appear later for dinner with his wife. I have also found it necessary from time to time to warn a regular customer, as he arrives with his new girlfriend, that his recently divorced and still bitter ex-wife is already in the restaurant. This situation can sometimes lead to what the police commonly refer to as 'a domestic'. We have even had the classic situation where a man came in with a woman other than his wife at the same time that his son-in-law pitched up with someone other than his daughter!

Not that Harry Rhodes himself has ever seemed in the least concerned about that kind of thing. All three of his wives, and quite a few girlfriends in between, have been wined and dined here. So, too, have three different mothers-in-law! Think about that!!

Harry owns and runs Tudor Photography in Banbury and we first got to know him shortly after we arrived at The Butcher's Arms. We were looking for someone to take pictures of the new bar following the completion of our early alterations and a friend recommended Harry. He did a great job and has been coming here ever since, both as a customer and in a professional capacity.

The official photographer at a number of big wedding receptions that have been held in the restaurant, he has also done a lot of publicity shoots here for various people. As a freelance newspaper cameraman, he has photographed everybody from the Queen to

Marlene Dietrich and from Muhammad Ali and Henry Cooper to The Beatles and The Rolling Stones and he has got a fund of fantastic stories as a result.

Among the photographs on the wall of the coffee lounge is one he recently presented to us of himself in a typically jaunty pose, with the inscription: '1973 – 11 stone, 2002 – 16 stone. Happy Eatings!' I fear we may have been at least partly responsible for a similar transformation in quite a few of our regular customers.

The Love Nest, which I reserve for Harry and his dinner dates and any other couples that I think might appreciate a quiet, romantic setting, has proven aphrodisiac properties. One delighted couple revealed to me that they had been trying unsuccessfully for a baby for seventeen years, only for the wife then to conceive on the very night that they had been seated at 14A for dinner. So, be warned!

The way in which the Love Nest came about also provides the background for a story that I tell against myself. It is built into what used to be a large Inglenook fireplace until I suddenly got the idea of blocking off the chimney and turning it into a cosy little alcove. As usual, no sooner had the thought formed in my mind than it was a case of out with the sledgehammer immediately after lunch one Sunday afternoon, in with builder Colin Amor and the job was completed virtually overnight, ready for normal business to be resumed on the Monday.

We had carefully shrouded the area in plastic sheets to protect the rest of the dining room from the clouds of flying dust while we were working and all that remained to be done the next morning was to clean up all the mess and debris, including the soot that had fallen from the chimney as we were knocking it about. I duly ventured in with the vacuum cleaner and after a few minutes was satisfied that I had made a pretty good job of clearing up every speck. It was only when I emerged from behind the plastic sheeting that I realised to my horror that I had forgotten to put a dust bag into the hoover and that everything had been blowing straight out of the back, covering the entire dining room in a thick film of soot.

With less than an hour to go before the first customers were due to start arriving for lunch it was a complete disaster.

I suppose that just about the worst crisis you can possibly have to deal with in a restaurant is for someone to drop dead at the table. This did actually happen to us once when an elderly man collapsed and died of a heart attack. Thankfully, we were able to handle things in a way that caused a minimum amount of upset to those around him. Some people present had no idea that anything particularly untoward had happened.

There was one other occasion when a woman collapsed and had to be rushed to hospital, but what was remarkable about that was the fact that once the ambulance had taken her off with sirens blaring and lights flashing, her husband returned to the table as if nothing had happened and calmly finished his meal. Mind you, he had always been a bit of a character. A bomber pilot during the war, he was still regularly flying a light aircraft in his seventies and was mourned at his funeral by no less than three different girlfriends!

Peter always takes great delight in citing the catastrophic hoovering of the Love Nest as an example of my general domestic ineptitude. This was again on display when an electrical fault in the main fuse box out the back caused the current to arc alarmingly, starting a small fire in the early hours of what just happened to be Bonfire Night. With electricity sparking and crackling all over the place I rushed out and, without thinking, was about to start spraying everything with water from a hand-held fire extinguisher. Thankfully, Peter spotted me at the last moment and, realising what I was about to do, jumped forward and knocked it out of my hand before I got what could have been a very nasty shock!

I have to admit that I am by no means the world's most practical individual. In the same way, I have occasionally found it difficult to grasp the everyday complexities of public transport. Augusta and I used to go up to London every year for the Chelsea Flower Show and because we had begun to find parking increasingly difficult we decided it would be better to go by train from Rugby. Going up was fine. Coming back was the problem. The first time we did it we somehow managed to get on the wrong train and ended up in Crewe, having shot straight through Rugby without stopping.

I was determined not to make the same mistake the following year and yet, somehow, we once again contrived to end up in Crewe. I was dancing about on the platform, literally hopping mad, and when we eventually managed to find a porter I angrily demanded to know how long we would have to wait for a train back. The porter immediately pointed to one that was already standing at a platform on the other side of the station and said that if we hurried we might just catch it. Augusta and I raced across the bridge and threw ourselves into a carriage just as the guard blew his whistle. Our relief was short-lived, however. As we once again hurtled through Rugby at high speed it emerged that the train was non-stop all the way back to Euston! That was the last time we ever went to the Flower Show.

Thankfully, things tend to run much more smoothly in the restaurant, even if the atmosphere behind the scenes can sometimes be rather like it is backstage at a theatre five minutes before curtain up. Thankfully, none of our chefs has ever been particularly temperamental – apart from Augusta, that is! And even Augusta would always stop short of threatening people with meat cleavers in time-honoured fashion. Simon, our head chef for over twenty-five years, and his successors, Dion Van Overdijk, Albert Simao and, most recently, Adam Newman, a highly talented young chef who comes from Warwick, have all been brilliant, helping us to build our reputation for a perfectly-balanced traditional menu, with the finest ingredients cooked to a consistently high standard.

We can already claim to have had a hand in launching the career of one culinary superstar in Tony Tobin. One of the stars of TV's 'Ready, Steady, Cook', Tony grew up in Priors Marston and first got interested in cooking through working part-time in the kitchen at The Butcher's Arms. He actually spent most of his time here washing up and peeling potatoes but it was the experience of watching Simon and Augusta at work that inspired him to go to catering college. I actually bought him his first set of professional chef's knives when he started his training. Tony, who made his name when he went on to work for the legendary Nico Ladenis and who now has his own highly-rated restaurant, The Dining Room in Reigate, Surrey, has been back to eat here several times since and whenever he is interviewed he is always very generous with his compliments, going out of his way to mention the time he spent here and the encouragement we gave him.

Over the years we've also had several great personalities among our waiting staff of whom there are currently a total of twenty-four, twelve of them full-time, led by our extremely imposing restaurant manager Nuno Correia. The whole team are so good that it seems unfair to pick out individuals and yet Terri McGregor, the mistress of the sweet trolley, must have a special mention.

Terri, famed for the stylishly extrovert manner in which she dispenses the cream, has been offering temptation beyond endurance to even the most diet-conscious diners for more than thirty years. She arrived here in 1978 after being told by a friend that there might be a temporary part-time job going and she has been a permanent and very popular fixture ever since. There is one long-standing male customer who insists that his bald spot is the result of resting his head against Terri's ample bosom as she runs through the contents of her trolley of delights! There are also dark stories of bribes being offered to secure the last remaining portion whenever there's a run on the bread-and-butter pudding.

Nuno was preceded as head waiter by Steve Syvret. With us for over fifteen years before emigrating to Australia to set up his own restaurant, Steve was very popular with the customers and became a bit of a star when he made two separate appearances as a contestant on the TV quiz show 15 to 1. He also won the Midlands regional title as Sommelier of the Year in 2002 before going on to compete in the national finals.

Clearly a man of many and varied talents, he was also a goalkeeper to reckon with, despite his diminutive size, helping Portugal (as represented by The Butcher's Arms) to win a four nations five-a-side charity soccer tournament organised annually by Tracy Lennard in aid of Rugby's St Cross Hospital.

Playing against other restaurant teams representing Spain, Italy and England, we followed our Cup-winning triumph in 2000 with second place in 2001. Apart from Steve, our other secret weapon was waiter Orlando Martins, who just happened to be a relative of Portuguese international soccer star Jose Dominguez.

Of all the waiters we have had over the years, one of the most popular was a young man who had perhaps better remain nameless. A colourful character, he had an eye for the ladies, a weakness that was forever getting him into all sorts of scrapes. There was much jumping out of windows to escape irate returning husbands and boyfriends and whenever one got to hear of these escapades, he would always blame it all on 'Percy'. "It's true, Lino," he would confess, with a mischievous grin. "Percy has been out of control again!"

A fairly typical romantic escapade began with him and Steve Syvret having a drink together in the public bar on their Sunday evening off. He got chatting to a girl and, at closing time, persuaded her to accompany him back to his room in the staff quarters at the back of the building. Steve himself, meanwhile, retired to his room and was about to go to bed when he was woken by a knock on his door. It was his amorous young colleague. Had Steve by any chance got a bottle of wine he could let him have? He had. Had he perhaps also got two glasses? Yes, he had. "And one more thing Steve. Can you remember her name?" Despite all this, he was an immensely likeable chap. He was with us for quite a while before eventually leaving to go into the computer business where I believe that he has been enormously successful. Meanwhile, our customers still ask after him – especially the ladies.

Male customers, on the other hand, are perhaps more likely to remember Nadine, the waitress I literally 'picked up' during the

30-hour trip from Johannesburg to Cape Town on South Africa's fabulous Blue Train. Augusta and I were on holiday at the time with Derek Salt and his wife, another couple we had known since our Westgate days. Derek has had business interests in South Africa for many years and he and I alone had already enjoyed a fantastic ten-day holiday there in 1996, the highlights of which included a stay at the Mali Mali game reserve and a very moving visit to Robben Island, scene of Nelson Mandela's imprisonment.

At Mali Mali, on the edge of the Kruger National Park, we got to see the Big Five at very close quarters and there was an anxious moment as far as I was concerned when a very large lion suddenly advanced rather menacingly to within a few feet of our Land Rover, looked directly up at me and opened its mouth frighteningly wide! I really thought I was in danger of being attacked and eaten. Derek, of course, found the whole episode very amusing.

We also took the opportunity during the trip to visit some of the country's best hotels and restaurants, including the Grill Room at the Royal Hotel in Durban, the Zoo Lake restaurant in Johannesburg and the Mount Nelson hotel in Cape Town. Whenever I go away to places like this I always take a close professional interest in what they have to offer in case I can pinch a few ideas. At the Royal Hotel I was so impressed by their cheesecake that I got the chef to give me the recipe, which is the one we now use at The Butcher's Arms. At the Mount Nelson it was a special soup that I was interested in. And at the Zoo Lake I even tried, in vain, to get them to sell me their ornately carved sweet trolley.

It was when Derek and I returned to South Africa with our wives that I managed to secure Nadine's services. She was the butler assigned to our suite on the Blue Train, which included a bedroom, lounge and bathroom, and I was so impressed with her wonderful personality and the brilliant way she did her job that I asked if she would consider coming to work for us in Priors Hardwick. It then turned out that she was actually looking for an excuse to spend some time in England and was delighted to take me up on the offer.

Unfortunately, she was only able to be with us for a few months.

During another holiday with the Salts, this time in Switzerland, I again tried to poach a waitress who was serving us, only for my plans to be scuppered on this occasion by Augusta. The girl was an absolute cracker, unbelievably sexy just in the way she moved around the restaurant. I whispered to Derek: "If we had her at The Butcher's Arms the place would be packed every night!" Augusta took one look at her and said very firmly: "No way!" So, that was the end of that idea.

As we moved into the mid-nineties, our fame spread along with the signed pictures of VIP customers on the walls of the restaurant. These now included everyone from American astronaut Colonel Tom Stafford – brought here by former Rover Group manufacturing director Andrew Barr, who had met him through business contacts in America – right through to 'Big Ron' Atkinson, former football manager and then a TV commentator until an indiscreet remark uttered when he thought the microphone was switched off ended his broadcasting career.

Ron was one of a succession of Coventry managers who have come here over the years, starting with Jimmy Hill. It was in the restaurant here that the club chairman at the time, Derek Robbins, promised Jimmy a large amount of money out of his own pocket to buy the players that Jimmy reckoned they needed to put Coventry in what was then the First Division. And when they duly won promotion, they had the celebration party here, as they did on a later occasion when Roland Nilsson was named Manager of the Month.

Jimmy used to be a regular here during his time with Coventry and we have since been told the story of how, some years later, he was stopped in London by a traffic cop on suspicion of some minor traffic offence, only to be waved on his way as soon as he was recognised by the patrolman who told him: "You probably won't remember, sir, but the last time we met was when you bought me a drink in The Butcher's Arms."

Augusta's nephew Eric had a similar experience when he was working for us in the early days. He was dating the daughter of a high-ranking local police officer at the time and she happened to be with him in his car when he was picked up for speeding one night. The traffic cop who had pulled him over was just about to book him when he suddenly recognised who was sitting in the passenger seat, whereupon he stepped back smartly and saluted! Those were the days!

Another well-known name who has become a regular customer and a great friend of the family in recent years is someone whose face few people would probably recognise – haulage boss Eddie Stobart or Edward, as he prefers to be called. Yet again, it was Tony Mason who introduced him to us. Tony had done a television interview with Edward after his distinctive trucks, with their handsome green, red and gold livery, had rather surprisingly attracted a cult following. As a result of that interview he was then asked to appear in a 60-minute promotional video for the company and the two became friendly.

Tony brought him to the restaurant for dinner one day after the opening of a new depot at Crick, near Rugby and he enjoyed himself so much that he then started coming with his family. We got to know him well and at one point he invited us up with Peter and Helen and the grandchildren for a guided tour of the new depot. The kids were allowed to scramble all over the trucks, each of them famously identified with a girl's name painted on the cab, before being presented with scale models from the range that are much sought after by members of what is perhaps one of the world's unlikeliest fan clubs.

Meanwhile, with Peter himself happily settled in the new house and taking an ever more important role in running the business, everything seemed to be going wonderfully well. Then, out of the blue, we found ourselves facing a situation that threatened to leave both the family and the business in ruins.

A FIGHT FOR SURVIVAL

On the evening of February 1st, 1998, the car park at The Butcher's Arms started to fill up with an even more glittering array than usual of Rolls Royces, Bentleys, Mercedes, Aston Martins, Ferraris, Porsches, Jaguars and other top-of-the-range models as around one hundred of our best customers arrived for what was to be one of the happiest nights we've ever had here.

Billed as The Royal Marsden Charity Evening Auction, we had laid it on primarily as a special fund-raising thank you to consultant Dr (now Professor) David Cunningham and all his staff at the world famous cancer hospital where Peter had just been successfully treated. For us, as a family, it was a chance not only to show our gratitude for everything that had been done for Peter but also to celebrate the end of a nightmare that, for a while, had threatened to overwhelm us.

It had begun with nothing more than backache. Despite regular weekly visits to osteopaths, chiropractors and physiotherapists over a period of many months, Peter found that this was gradually becoming more and more severe until, by Christmas 1996, he was living permanently on painkillers while struggling to get through his day's work. He went to see further specialists but still the problem was put down to a possible slipped disc.

It was towards the end of May 1997 that it started to become clear that we were dealing with something much more serious. Augusta and I were away for the weekend with old friends Derek Salt and his wife, celebrating my 64th birthday with a trip to France and Switzerland that included a special tour of Moet and Chandon in Rheims laid on by former Formula 2 racing driver Robin Widdows, another good friend and regular customer who now works for Moet as a public relations executive. We found out only after we got back to Priors Hardwick that Peter had been sent to hospital on the Sunday with a badly swollen leg, which our GP, Peter Middleton, had suspected might be a thrombosis. Peter Middleton dispatched him to the Horton Hospital in Banbury where he sat in Accident and Emergency for two hours waiting to have a blood test, only to be told that his sample couldn't be analysed until the following day because it was a Bank Holiday.

The results, when they did eventually come through, again showed nothing significant. At this point it was thought that the problem might be due to a blocked lymph gland and he was sent to see another specialist who prescribed massage in an effort to reduce the swelling. At the same time, the leg was bandaged from hip to ankle.

None of this did the slightest good and Peter continued to go downhill, although he never complained and did his best to carry on working as normal. Things eventually came to a head a few weeks later in July. Augusta had gone off to the villa in Portugal for a few days and, as I often did when she was away, I arranged to take Peter and the family for a Chinese meal in Southam early on the Sunday evening. However, when I went round to pick them up I found Peter slumped in his chair, looking absolutely drained. He made no mention of the Chinese meal but simply asked me if I would mind taking the kids to school the next morning. I was obviously very concerned and asked him if he was OK. As usual, he just pulled a face and said he wasn't feeling great but not to worry, the back was playing him up but he would have an early night and would soon be fine.

Peter has a small sideline storing classic cars for people and when I went to pick the kids up on the Monday morning he was on the telephone to one of his clients and I overheard him say quietly: "I'm afraid I can't see you today, I am not a well man." That was the first time I had heard him admit as much and at that moment I knew it was time to take drastic action. I went straight out to my car, called Peter Middleton on my mobile phone and told him bluntly: "Peter, my son is very ill. I am about to take his children in to school and I want him in hospital by the time I get home again."

I was still on the road when the doctor rang me back to confirm that he had been to see Peter, that he was indeed very poorly and that an ambulance was on its way to take him to Banbury's private Foscote Hospital. There, three days later, a surgeon carried out the operation that revealed the presence of a tumour.

Nothing can prepare you for a shock like that. We were then told that the appropriate course of treatment could not be decided until the results of a biopsy and various other tests came through. The next few days seemed like eternity as we waited for the tests and scans to be carried out one by one, feeling increasingly helpless as we watched Peter fading in front of our eyes. By the following Monday evening he was clearly very, very poorly and there was an awful moment when Helen and Augusta had left the room and he took my hand and whispered: "Dad, please look after my kids." It was in that highly charged, emotional instant that I once again realised that I would have to seize the initiative and get things moving if my son was to have any chance of survival.

I don't read a lot of books, but one that had happened to catch my attention and which I had then found I couldn't put down was former Champion Jockey Bob Champion's inspirational account of his fight against cancer and of how he recovered to win the Grand National. Most of all, I remembered that it was the treatment he received at the Royal Marsden hospital that had saved him.

I rang Peter Middleton that evening and said: "I want you to help me make the necessary arrangements because, whatever anyone says, tomorrow morning I am going to take my son to the hospital where they cured Bob Champion." He was quite taken aback. He said: "Lino, you can't do it just like that." I told him: "You just watch me."

When he realised just how determined I was, he called the Royal Marsden, arranged for an emergency admission and said that he would organise an ambulance for nine o'clock the next morning.

At the appointed hour we were all waiting there – me, Augusta, Helen and Helen's parents – but 9.00 a.m. came and went and by ten o'clock there was still no sign of the ambulance. I contacted Peter Middleton to find out what was happening and after making a check call he rang back, very apologetically, to say that he had now been told that an ambulance could not be provided that morning. He offered, instead, to drive us to the Marsden himself in Peter's own Range Rover. And that's exactly what happened.

Peter is a big man and, with all his various drips attached, just getting him out of his wheelchair and into the front seat of the Range Rover was no easy job. We eventually managed it and with Peter Middleton driving and myself, Helen and a nurse in the back we eventually headed off up the motorway.

For all of us that two-hour journey was the most terrible ordeal, but for Peter himself, by now desperately ill, it must have been unimaginably awful. At one point I noticed that we had turned off the M25 and were going past Heathrow and I asked Peter Middleton if he was sure he knew exactly where he was going. It turned out he was heading for the Royal Marsden in Fulham and I had to tell him: "That's not the right place. I want the Royal Marsden in Sutton, Surrey – that's where Bob Champion was treated." So we turned back at the next exit and went on to Sutton. Peter told me much later that he remembered thinking when told that we were going to be delayed for another fifteen minutes that he actually might not be able to make it. That's how desperate things had become.

There is no doubt in my mind that, but for the Royal Marsden, Peter would not still be with us today. From the moment we stepped through the doors it was obvious that we were in the very best possible hands. Instantly, it was as if everything had gone into overdrive. I stayed with Peter until ten o'clock that night and by then he was already being prepared for his first cocktail of chemotherapy drugs. Within hours of our arrival, the team looking after him had scanned his entire body, had carried out all the necessary tests and had got the results back so that they knew exactly what the problem was and what sort of treatment was required. That is the kind of fast-track care you routinely get at what is rightly renowned as the finest cancer research centre in the world.

Professor Cunningham confirmed that Peter was suffering from a particular type of Non-Hodgkin's Lymphoma and was able to give us a little bit of encouragement by explaining that although a highly aggressive cancer, it was also potentially curable.

One of their initial concerns was that Peter's kidneys would not be able to cope with the powerful cocktail of drugs that they felt were necessary in his case. As soon as she heard this Helen offered, without hesitation, to donate one of her own kidneys if necessary. That was another moment that I will never forget. It explains why I always tell people: "As far as I am concerned, I don't just have a son and a daughter-in-law – I have a son and a daughter."

The next three months were a blurr of stress and exhaustion, both physical and emotional, punctuated by highs and lows of hope and anxiety. They say that it is at times like this that you discover who your real friends are and we very soon found that we were blessed with a huge number of the best and truest friends anyone could ever wish for.

Our regular customers, in particular, were fantastic. Without exception, they all rallied round and shared everything with us, always wanting to know how Peter was getting on and often providing much-needed shoulders to cry on while Peter himself was flooded with cards and letters from around the world as the word spread.

Nor was it just a matter of morale support. Many people went out of their way to offer practical assistance. For instance, Augusta and Helen had moved into family accommodation at the hospital so that one or other or both of them could always be at Peter's bedside, but I stayed at home to run the business, travelling up every morning to visit him for a couple of hours before work. This involved leaving Priors Hardwick at 6.00 a.m. and then returning in time to open up for lunch at noon. And because I was anxious about driving myself when I was tired and with my mind full of so many other distractions, I soon had customers volunteering to chauffeur me there and back. There was a whole rota of people who were prepared to get up at 5.00 a.m. and sometimes even earlier so that they could be ready to pick me up at six, sharp.

Among the many who helped out in this way, Tim Pearson was especially generous with his time. A highly successful businessman, now semi-retired, Tim is another customer who, over the years, has become a close personal friend, even, for a while, owning a villa next door to ours in Portugal. Throughout the entire time that Peter was in hospital, Tim rang me every evening to make sure I was all right and to offer himself as a driver for the next morning.

Those who went out of their way to visit included Terry Lister, who runs the biggest independent group of garages in the country. Terry, from whom Peter has bought a fair few cars over the years, took time out from his very busy schedule to drive up to Sutton. On arrival, he found that his Bentley wouldn't fit into a single car parking space so he had to pay for two. He has always enjoyed a light-hearted relationship with Peter and when he walked into his hospital room he brandished the two parking tickets and told Peter: "You owe me £2 for these! I don't want it now but make sure you give it to me next time you see me in the restaurant." It was Terry's way of boosting Peter's morale by showing that he had no doubt that things would soon be back to normal. In the meantime, he also presented Peter with two fabulous illustrated books about Formula 1. Six months later, Peter was to take great delight in handing over the two quid.

The fantastic support system so generously provided by my friends and customers was what kept me going through those dark days when we still weren't sure how things were going to turn out. I found that as long as I was busy in the restaurant I was OK. It was when everybody had gone home and I was left alone at night that terrible thoughts would inevitably start to race through my mind.

It was three weeks after our frantic dash to the Royal Marsden that we saw the first glimmer of light at the end of the tunnel. David Cunningham called us together and explained that the tumour, which was inoperable because it was too close to the diaphragm, had been shrunk by the initial bout of chemotherapy from the size of a football to that of a walnut. Quietly spoken, with a soft Scottish accent, David's calm and authoritative manner had inspired confidence right from the start. "I think Peter's going to be all right," he said.

This marvellous news was followed a few days later by another emotional moment when, in the family room at the hospital, little James took his first steps, tottering uncertainly to the side of the bed. Peter was still very ill and weak from the massive doses of drugs he was being fed but managed a little smile before turning away five minutes later and asking us to leave, exhausted by the strain. There was still a long way to go.

Altogether he had six separate courses of chemotherapy over a four-month period during which he was in and out of hospital. He lost all his hair, more than ten stone in weight and most of his muscle power. He was so wasted at the end of the treatment that he was in a wheelchair and virtually had to learn to walk all over again.

He came home for the first time just before his wedding anniversary on August 19th. That had been one of the targets he set himself once he started to recover. He told the doctors that whatever happened he had to be back for that and, realising how important it was for him psychologically to be able to keep that date, they let him out for a few days 'on parole', even though his treatment was by no means complete.

Each bout of chemotherapy normally involves a three-week cycle. It doesn't affect you too badly in the first week but as the chemo kicks in you feel terrible in the middle week. The body's natural immune system is then supposed to pick you up again in the third week so that you are well enough for the next bout. Peter, however, had become so debilitated that he found he was going downhill all the way after the first week and therefore had to spend the last ten days of each cycle back in hospital so that they could help him get his strength back.

As he gradually started to improve, Peter had another target in his sights. Before all this had happened, he and his best friend Greg Hobbs had booked tickets for a Phil Collins concert at the NEC at the end of November and he was determined to be fit enough to go. Greg, who lives and works in America, had phoned him regularly from the States while he was still in hospital and had done a wonderful job of keeping his spirits up, constantly egging him on by saying: "You've got to get better before November because we don't want to miss Phil Collins."

His final discharge from the Royal Marsden came on November 5th. Even then he was still in no fit state for any major celebrations so, although we were obviously delighted and hugely relieved to see him back, it was a fairly low-key welcome home. He had lost so much weight that his clothes were literally falling off him and this led to a moment of light relief that helped everybody to smile and relax a little. Helen had employed a nanny called Juliet to help her mother look after the children while she herself was spending so much time at the hospital and one of the things that stands out in Peter's memory of his homecoming is that as he got out of the Range Rover and Juliet stepped forward to be introduced to him, his trousers suddenly dropped to his ankles.

Later that day there was then another very emotional moment when he called Greg in America to tell him that he was back and would definitely be able to make it to the concert. Halfway through the conversation Greg suddenly stopped talking. "Hello? Hello? Are you still there?" asked Peter. "Yes," replied Greg, after a few seconds' silence. "I'm still here. Sorry about that. I'm just so happy to hear your voice back to normal that I can't stop crying."

As a family, we all felt very much the same. It had been the most terrible six months imaginable, particularly for Helen and Augusta who had lived with the pressure twenty-four hours-a-day, seven-days-a-week, right from the start. As Peter himself says, he was so heavily drugged, especially during those tense early stages, that he didn't know that much about what was going on a lot of the time. For Helen and Augusta there had been no such escape from the relentless emotional stress of having to sit by helplessly while a loved one fights for survival.

I have been lucky so far in my life, winning all the battles. But there were times when I feared that we were not going to win this one. That we were able to do so was due almost entirely to David Cunningham and his team at the Royal Marsden. We were enormously grateful and wanted to say thank you in a significant way and gradually the idea of a £200-a-head auction dinner in aid of the hospital took shape.

With our amazing customer base, we were confident that we could organise something fairly special but even so we were amazed by the response we got when we started writing to people asking if there was anything they could donate as an auction prize. We were immediately bombarded with the most fantastic offers. Included among them were the use of a Jaguar XK8 Sports Convertible for three months, a two week holiday in a six-bedroom house overlooking a championship golf course in Florida, a week for two in a lakeside hotel near Chicago, with air flights and a hire car thrown in, two grandstand seats for the 1998 British Grand Prix at Silverstone and two complete Coventry City soccer strips plus two match balls autographed by the players. Altogether we had around forty very varied items.

As far as we were concerned, there was only one man to conduct the auction – David Hobbs. If anybody was going to be able to take the Mickey out of our customers and still draw the funds, it was David. He flew over specially from America and, just as we knew he would, did an absolutely magnificent job, helping us to raise more money than we had ever thought possible, even in our wildest dreams.

The atmosphere on the night was fantastic. David Cunningham

was there, as were Senior Registrar Gary Middleton and Senior House Officer Michael Bayne, the two young doctors who had dealt with Peter on a daily basis throughout his stay in the Royal Marsden and with whom he had forged a special rapport. An extremely busy man, Professor Cunningham's commitments meant that he couldn't get away from the hospital until quite late and we were a bit anxious that he might not be able to get to us in time until Tony Rutter, sales manager at Speeds, the Stratford-upon-Avon Mercedes Benz dealers, very kindly offered to drive him down in person. A close friend of Peter's, to whom he proudly claims to have sold a car from every dealership he has ever worked for, Tony whisked the doctor through the evening rush hour traffic in the supercharged Jaguar XJR that was Peter's pride and joy at the time.

Excitement mounted as we got to the end of the meal in the packed restaurant and the main business of the evening got under way, with David Hobbs whipping up enthusiasm for the auction in his usual inimitable style. First up was a sterling silver desk clock from Fred Burrow of Gurit Essex, which got us off to a flying start with a winning bid of £550. This was followed by £500 for 'The Gates of Althorp, Vision of Heaven', an original water colour donated by writer Ted Elkins and his wife.

The XK8, donated by Nick Scheele, then Chairman of Jaguar, was knocked down for £3,000 to a couple who used it to tour Europe in style, while the house in Florida, donated by David Hobbs himself, fetched the same amount. In addition, David got together with John Sadiq to offer a week's holiday at Elkhart Lake, near Chicago, including flights and a car, which went for £1,500. The grandstand seats at Silverstone were bought for £800 and the Coventry FC kits for £700.

And so it went on. A day's off-road instruction at Land Rover's jungle track at Solihull and a day driving a new MGF at a racing circuit, both kindly donated by John Parkinson of the Rover Group, went for £500 and £300 respectively and a tour of Prodrive's World

Championship winning rally team headquarters and a tour of the Benetton Formula 1 factory donated by David Richards and David Lapworth of Prodrive also brought in £500.

A tour of the Aston Martin factory at Newport Pagnell, followed by a drive around the Goodwood race circuit in a new DB7 and the use of the car for a further four days attracted a winning bid of £800 and a week's stay in a Cornish country cottage donated by Jenny Hayward was snapped up for the same amount. Somebody paid £750 to have their kitchen floor tiled in marble, donated by Don Bannocks of Bannock's Tigre Marble, £650 secured a day's racing for three people at Donington Park in a Caterham 7, courtesy of Andrew and Stuart Parker of Team Parker racing, and a beautiful Portuguese crochet table cloth, hand-made by Augusta, made £1,200. An eight-bottle Imperial of Grahams 1985 vintage port, donated by us, was knocked down to Nick Scheele for £1,500 only for him to give it straight back for re-auction whereupon it fetched a further £1,200.

The highest prices of the evening were paid for two all-expenses paid weekends at our villa in Portugal, with Augusta and I as hosts. Originally, the plan was to offer only one weekend but that all changed after Michael Rosenberg, who couldn't be present at the dinner as he was once again cruising on the QE2, made what we all thought would be a pre-emptive bid, in advance, of $10,000 (£6,300).

We never thought for one moment that anybody would be prepared to top such a handsome offer but then, on the night, garage chain owner David Holmes, another favourite customer and good friend, amazed everybody by raising it to £7,500. In the circumstances, we felt that we couldn't possibly disappoint Michael so we simply arranged a second weekend. It has to be said that this was not too much of a hardship, especially when Michael, in characteristically generous style, insisted on paying for Augusta and I to join him and his wife on the QE2 for the voyage back from Lisbon.

When all the figures were finally totted up, they showed that the grand total raised during the evening amounted to over £82,250. David Cunningham was quite stunned. He said that he had been to a similar fund-raising event in London's Guildhall where only a fraction of that amount had been raised despite the fact that on that occasion there had been 500 people present.

He wrote me a charming letter of thanks afterwards in which he said: "I can barely find the words to describe how appreciative we all are here of the enormous efforts that went into raising the substantial sum of £82,262.50 for the research fund. This was an incredible act of generosity and reflected the incredible commitment on your part to the Celebration Dinner and the amazing generosity from your friends and patrons of the Butcher's Arms."

And he added: "When it came to the auction, the speed of the bidding and the sums involved were absolutely breathtaking. All of this has led to a major donation which will facilitate further research into the treatment of lymphoma, so that hopefully in the future all patients with this condition can look forward to a normal life expectancy."

Peter was soon able to demonstrate his own return to normality to Professor Cunningham in a rather appropriate manner. Towards the end of his stay in the Marsden, Helen was pushing him around the grounds in his wheelchair on a warm summer's day when he noticed a silver Aston Martin DB7 in the staff car park with the letters DC in the registration. "I bet that's David Cunningham's car," he told Helen. From then on he couldn't stop talking about how beautiful it was and how he was going to have one just like it himself once he was better.

A few months after he finally came out of hospital he did indeed acquire one that was exactly the same and when the time came for his next six-monthly check-up, he took great delight in driving himself up to the Royal Marsden in it. As I watched him roar off up the lane it seemed to me in a way to symbolise his recovery. There could be no clearer indication that my car-crazy son was back to his old self.

HEART OF THE COMMUNITY

On January 1st, 1998, just a month before the Auction Dinner for the Royal Marsden, we had marked the 25th anniversary of our arrival at The Butcher's Arms with a special celebration lunch party for our village pensioners. Of the thirty who came along, several were well into their eighties. Most had already been living in Priors Hardwick for many years before we moved in and one or two had actually been born in the village.

It was an occasion for much nostalgic reminiscence. The late Mary Winn, who ran the village post office from her home for forty years before retiring in 1994 at the age of 82, remembered collecting her water in a bucket from a spring in the church wall, just as Augusta had been doing in Paiágua at around the same time. And Mrs Muriel Clements, seventy-four years old in 1998, recalled her father making his living as a smallholder from small patches of land scattered in and around the village, much as my parents had done in Vinha. "To leave the village was a big event in those days," said Muriel, reminding me once again of what life used to be like in rural Portugal during my childhood.

Not all the talk was about "the good old days". People remembered how, in 1959, the *Sunday Mercury* newspaper published a feature under the headline 'A Village Comes To The End Of The Road' in which it was reported that Priors Hardwick was a dying community, with the school reduced to six pupils and about to close down, the village shop also on the verge of shutting for good and the 14th-century church – its stained glass windows once singled out for praise by famed architectural historian Sir Nicholas Pevsner – in danger of collapse. The Butcher's Arms itself faced closure with a spokesman for the Flowers brewery quoted as saying: "Takings aren't very high –its future is very, very undecided."

Forty years later, in 1999, the *Birmingham Post* devoted a whole page to a feature article headlined 'Feast Of Life At Doomed Village' that paid tribute to "the Portuguese restaurateur who put a tiny English village back on the map". It pointed out that during a busy summer weekend upwards of five hundred people came to eat at The Butcher's Arms, more than double the entire population of Priors Hardwick.

The reporter was suitably impressed by the fact that on the day he came in our customers just happened to include Edward Wilson, the Professor who had worked out Apollo 11's route to the moon for NASA, ventriloquist Ray Alan, creator of Lord Charles, and Jim Randall, the man who designed Jaguar's V12 engine. As he noted in his article – not quite the selection of people you would normally expect to find sharing the dining room of village pub in a fairly remote corner of Warwickshire.

I was especially proud of that particular bit of unsolicited publicity. It came in the same week as the announcement that Nick Scheele was leaving Jaguar to take over Ford UK. That was very big industrial news in the Midlands, but on the Saturday that our feature appeared Nick rang me to complain jokingly: "How come I only rate a few paragraphs and you've got a whole page!"

Monica Lewinsky, the White House intern at the heart of the sex scandal involving former American president Bill Clinton, was in Birmingham that week and even she got fewer column inches than The Butcher's Arms! Fame indeed.

Looking back over our time in Priors Hardwick, I am proud to think that we have played a part in reviving the village. We certainly gave it a new heart. And although one or two of the crustier locals weren't too thrilled at first about the idea of having a thriving business in their midst, our arrival was welcomed by most people. Also, I don't think there is much doubt that our presence has helped to attract the sort of residents who have moved in and done up many of the older properties, turning this into one of the most sought-after addresses in the area.

At the same time, we have done our best to get involved in the community at every level, whether providing free Christmas dinners for village pensioners, twice funding the restoration of St Mary's church or simply supporting local initiatives such as the hugely successful Priors School venture. Masterminded by David and Judith Adams and other residents of Priors Marston, this wonderfully ambitious project involved rescuing the village school from threatened closure by raising enough money to reopen it as the country's first privately funded primary school.

At one point a special fund-raising dinner was organised at The Butcher's Arms at which Earl Spencer was the guest of honour and afterwards he sent me a charming hand-written letter of thanks that takes pride of place in our scrapbook. The Earl's father also used to come to the restaurant quite regularly and, on one occasion, actually invited me to a dinner party at Althorp. Unfortunately, it was to be held on a Saturday, the busiest night of the week for us, and as this was before Peter had joined us and could stand in for me if necessary, I felt that I had to decline. That decision remains one of the greatest regrets of my life because I found out later that the guest list also included the Queen. I'm sure that The Butcher's Arms would have survived my absence for just one Saturday night and, as it was, I missed a fantastic, once-in-a-lifetime chance to meet Her Majesty.

By way of consolation, I have had the honour of dining at various times with both former Portuguese Prime Minister Mario Soares and ex-President Jorge Sampaio while they were still in office.

My encounter with the President took place during his visit to London in early 2002. I was one of just twenty representatives from the expatriate Portuguese community in the UK who were specially invited by the Ambassador to attend a dinner in his honour at the Guildhall.

I met Mario Soares, who was President for ten years from 1986 to 1996, at a lunch in Leicester after he had been presented with an honorary degree by Leicester University. I managed to have a long chat with him, during which I was able to tell him how much I had admired him and how much I sympathised with him for the years he spent in exile during the dictatorship. I made the point that I knew just how difficult that must have been for him because, just like him but for very different reasons, I, too, had gone for years without seeing my family after I left Portugal in 1960. He then became very chatty and we spoke for about twenty minutes after which he invited me to go and see him at his home in Portugal next time I was there. So far, I have not had the right opportunity to take him up on that but maybe I will eventually.

I also felt extremely honoured to find myself seated next to former British Prime Minister John Major at a special Gala Evening organised by the local Conservative Association in memory of the late Lord Prentice of Daventry. I was especially proud because most of the VIP guests present at the Hellidon Lakes Hotel on that occasion were my customers, all of them very impressed to see me sitting next to such an illustrious Guest of Honour!

I had donated dinner for four at The Butcher's Arms as one of the items to be included in the fund-raising auction that took place during the evening and just to round off what was undoubtedly one of the more memorable occasions of my life, this fetched considerably more than a similar item offered by rivals Fawsley Hall! I was in such a good mood that I immediately made the winning bid for a beautiful bouquet of roses, which I then made a point of presenting to Constituency President Lady Hesketh.

While I'm name-dropping, I might as well mention that on another memorable occasion I found myself sitting down to dinner with Bill Clinton, Boris Yeltsin, Tony Blair and several other world leaders. It happened when they were all in Birmingham for the G8 world economic conference in 1998, during which Bill Clinton was famously pictured enjoying a pint of bitter in one of the bars down by the canal. He and all the other big names were present at a special Media Party held in the International Convention Centre, to which I had very kindly been invited by the late David Perry, Sales

Director of Bablake Wines at the time, who had a table there.

Bablake's have been our main wine suppliers since the very early days and David was a good friend. I especially remember him taking me on a marvellous trip to Nuits-Saint-Georges one year to collect the Beaujolais Nouveau. There I was introduced to Jean-Claude Boisset, not just the biggest negotiant in the Burgundy region but a major figure in the wine industry worldwide. One funny little incident that stands out in my memory of that trip is that I happened to be wearing one of my special, extremely colourful ties at the time and Jean-Claude – clearly a man of exquisite taste! – admired it so much that I took it off and gave it to him on the spot.

Back at Priors Hardwick, other charity events at The Butcher's Arms over recent years have included a dinner and auction that produced £4,000 for the national Breakthrough Breast Cancer, a garden party and auction that raised £3,000 for the NSPCC and several raffle dinners that brought in a further £60,000 between them for the Royal Marsden.

The first raffle prize was a large working model of a forklift truck, specially made for us entirely out of wood by a former Rover car engineer who became a toymaker when he retired. That fetched £4,000. A beautiful doll's house raised £14,000. But the biggest fund-raiser was the miniature Ferrari Formula 1 racing car that I had originally bought as a birthday present for my grandson, Edward, after seeing it featured on the television show Blue Peter. Petrol driven and capable of 50 mph, it was a beautifully hand-made scale replica of the real thing but Edward, having rather outgrown it, was very happy to let us raffle it in such a good cause.

The car remained on display in the foyer for a year, during which time we managed to sell no fewer than 4,100 tickets at £10-a-time. I say 'we' but a lot of the credit has to go to Terri McGregor who must have been personally responsible for a large proportion of those sales. Ruthlessly exploiting the power and influence that she wields from her position in charge of the sweet trolley, she unashamedly dispensed special favours to customers prepared to buy yet another ticket in return for a slightly more generous helping of trifle. "Bread and butter pudding, sir? I'll see if we can find one more portion in the kitchen. In the meantime, how many raffle tickets was it that you wanted?"

Despite a very heavy schedule, Professor Cunningham himself found time once again to come down and make the draw personally during a special dinner on November 27th, 2001. Accompanied by his wife, he was driven up and down from London by freelance chauffeur John Morgan, who very generously offered his services free of charge for the evening.

When the winning ticket was drawn the winner of the ultimate little boy racer's dream car turned out to be a careful 29-year-old lady driver! Travel company sales manager Paula Needham had bought the winning ticket several months earlier when she came to dinner as part of a corporate hospitality event organised at Silverstone by one of the Grand Prix teams. "I'm so excited – it's the first time in my life that I've ever won anything," she said when she was rung at home to be given the news.

A wonderfully bubbly character, she added that she was not quite sure what she was going to do with it. "At five-foot-nine I'm afraid I'm a bit too big to drive it myself. I'm not married and don't have any children of my own but I do have three little nephews who will no doubt be able to enjoy it when they're a bit older. In the meantime I'll have to park it in my mum's double garage – next to her Fiesta!" Paula revealed that she herself drove a company BMW with the personalised number plate L4DY P. "It would look much better on a Ferrari, wouldn't it?" she sighed.

We were just delighted to have further boosted our total donation to the hospital, which then stood at £130,000 but which has since gone on to reach well over £300,000 thanks to the proceeds from the first two editions of this book and from Augusta's biography, *Life, Love and Food*. After everything that Professor Cunningham and his team had done for Peter, we were determined to do as much as we could in return to show the true depth of our gratitude. And we gained great satisfaction from the knowledge that by raising substantial sums for the research fund we were perhaps helping to save other people's lives in the future.

It was at around this time that a very well known businessman, who now sits in the House of Lords, came to lunch at The Butcher's Arms and happened to mention to me that he'd been invited to make a presentation of some sort in connection with the Royal Marsden but had been unable to do it because he just didn't have the time. When I heard that I felt I had to tell him off, urging him never to refuse such an invitation again, if only because he could never be sure that he might not one day need the Royal Marsden to return the favour.

To illustrate this point I told him the story of Graham Stanton. Graham and his brother Mike, both of them successful businessmen with their own separate companies, are regular customers and Mike not only took a table at the Royal Marsden auction but also made a successful bid for two items, including over £1,000 for a weekend for two at the Palacio de Seteais hotel. By an awful coincidence, Graham was then diagnosed only a few months later with Non Hodgkins Lymphoma, just as Peter had been. We were able to put him in touch with Professor Cunningham for a second opinion as a result of which the course of treatment originally suggested was changed and he subsequently made a complete recovery.

As I pointed out to my noble friend, Mike Stanton probably never imagined when he did his bit at the auction to support the Royal Marsden that his own brother would so soon be able to benefit from the world-class cancer research and expertise that he was helping to fund. So be warned, I told him – and if they ever ring you again and ask you to do them a favour, drop everything else and do it, because you never know when you might be grateful for their help in return. His Lordship was obviously quite taken aback by the strength of my feelings on the subject, but I like to think that he took to heart what I had to say.

The dreadful irony of that conversation, however, was that

as things turned out it was actually to be me who, in the most desperate of circumstances, would very shortly find myself having to go to Professor Cunningham for help once again, only to find that this time even he could not be the saviour I was praying for.

THE FINAL BATTLE

In November 2003, Augusta I set off on what had become our regular annual late autumn visit to the villa in Portugal, relishing the prospect of a few days relaxation and the chance to enjoy a last bit of warm sunshine before returning to Priors Hardwick with our batteries re-charged in readiness for the pre-Christmas rush.

Augusta, as ever, was itching to get back to tending her beloved garden and we were both looking forward to seeing family and friends, possibly even finding time to get up to Paiágua to visit the folks there, including Augusta's sisters Maria Marques and Maria Santos. Sadly, however, we had barely arrived before the holiday was ruined by what seemed at first to be a relatively minor accident, but which could be seen in retrospect as having set in motion a chain of increasingly devastating events.

For some time, Augusta had been plagued by regular attacks of cramp in her legs, especially at night when she was in bed. To ease the pain, she would get up and stretch the affected leg, while supporting herself on the little retaining wall that runs on each side of the bed at home in Priors Hardwick. But when she had a sudden attack in the middle of that first night after arriving at the villa, she momentarily forgot where she was. As she lurched out of bed in agony, she reached out for the wall that wasn't there and, grabbing thin air, slumped down very heavily on her backside.

She landed right on the point of her coccyx and X-rays later revealed that she had actually fractured one of the vertebrae. As a result she was obviously in considerable pain and found it extremely difficult to get about. The flight back to England was especially uncomfortable for her and by the time we got home after what was supposed to have been a refreshing break she looked drained. Peter has always maintained that his mum was never quite the same again after that fall; because although the pain from that injury eased over the next few months, Augusta had meanwhile begun to become aware of a nagging abdominal discomfort.

She didn't think that much about it until early the following year when she and I travelled up to Scotland along with our long-time friend Dr Peter Middleton and his wife, Sue, to attend a 60th birthday party in honour of our mutual friend Andy McGill, a wealthy businessman and regular customer at The Butcher's Arms. Sue Middleton used to be a nurse and when, in the back of the car on the way up, Augusta happened to mention to her the symptoms she had been experiencing Sue insisted that she must speak to Peter about having herself properly checked out. Peter agreed that she needed to have the problem looked at sooner rather than later and, although he had already retired as our local GP by this time, he duly arranged for an abdominal scan to be carried out at the Foscote hospital in Banbury as soon as we got back.

Our worst fears were then confirmed when the scan revealed the existence of a tumour on the pancreas. Peter rang me as soon as he got the results and it was agreed that we should get in touch straightaway with Professor Cunningham at the Royal Marsden to let him know exactly what was going on. I knew that the Professor would do everything he could to help and, sure enough, he made immediate arrangements for Augusta to be admitted to the Royal Marsden, where she was put under the care of surgeon Mr Jeremy Thompson.

Peter first and now Augusta – I could hardly believe it. It seemed as if lightning truly had struck twice in the same place. And yet although this obviously came as the most terrible shock and left me reeling, I was still confident at that stage that with David Cunningham and his team looking after her Augusta would be O.K. and that with their help she would survive, just as Peter had done.

Over the next few months it really did seem that she was going to come through it all. Following a successful operation to remove the tumour and a course of chemotherapy featuring the latest anti-cancer drugs that mercifully did not produce the more severe side-effects such as total hair loss, Augusta went into remission and seemed to be on the mend. Although she tended to tire easily, there were times when she was almost back to being her old self.

She insisted on going back to work in the kitchen and the office and would pop into the restaurant for gossipy chats with her favourite customers, her distinctive giggle once again echoing around the room as she regaled them with one of her terrible jokes, the punch line of which would all too often be lost amid gales of her own laughter. She was still able to drive herself to the hairdressers in her Porsche, she resumed her occasional holiday trips to Portugal and, most important for her, she was able to spend more time with the grandchildren. For a while we all dared to believe that she might be in the clear.

Our rising hopes then suffered a dreadful setback in early 2006 when a routine scan revealed that although there had been no recurrence of the pancreatic cancer, the niggling but gradually worsening pain in the back of her thigh was actually caused by a sarcoma, a totally different type of cancer, quite unconnected with the original one.

As if all that were not worrying enough, the situation was then made even more stressful by the fact that both Peter and I were simultaneously hit with health problems of our own, to such an extent that at one point in the ensuing weeks all three of us ended up in hospital at the same time – Peter and Augusta at the Royal Marsden in Fulham Road, London and me at the John Radcliffe in Oxford.

I had not been feeling one hundred per cent well for a while, experiencing a recurrence of the angina symptoms that had necessitated the angioplasty back in 1989. I had further treatment in January 2006, but things were still not quite right. And then, one Sunday morning in March, I began to feel so faint and unwell that we actually rang the emergency services and I was rushed by ambulance to the John Radcliffe.

My consultant cardiologist and good friend Adrian Banning was waiting for me when I arrived there and I was admitted to the intensive care unit while tests were carried out. These established that there was no immediately life threatening problem but also revealed that the reason I was feeling faint was that I was suffering from anaemia caused by intestinal bleeding of some sort. It was to be quite a time before a whole series of further tests eventually pinpointed exactly what the trouble was, after which it was fairly quickly sorted out.

Meanwhile, my emergency admission to hospital had taken place on the very day that Augusta was due to go to London to be operated on for the removal of the sarcoma. Matters were further complicated by the fact that Peter had also started feeling unwell at the time, meaning that there was nobody available or fit enough to take Augusta up to the Lister hospital in Chelsea. It was at this critical juncture that John and Jan Allen, our wonderful next door neighbours since 1995, came to the rescue, kindly offering to drive Augusta to London via the John Radcliffe, where she was able to visit me briefly in intensive care on the way.

At the Lister the following day, top surgeon Professor Meirion Thomas successfully removed a melon-sized tumour from Augusta's leg. She was afterwards transferred to the Royal Marsden and during the next few days we chatted to each other over the phone from our respective hospital beds! Peter, meanwhile, had continued to feel unwell and had been booked into the Royal Marsden for a precautionary scan. And so it was that for a few hours all three of us found ourselves hospitalised

Peter's problem was a hangover from the very heavy chemotherapy that he had undergone as part of his cancer treatment in 1997. This had had the unfortunate side effect of leaving him more vulnerable than he would otherwise have been to chest infections and breathing difficulties and in this instance it turned out to be the start of a long bout of illness that lasted two years. During that time there were spells when he was in such a bad way and so completely exhausted that he was brought to a complete standstill for days on end, quite unable to work.

Those two dreadful years were the worst of my life, with both Augusta and Peter battling serious ill health, while I myself was far from being at my best. Behind the scenes, Nuno and the rest of the staff worked brilliantly to keep the restaurant running smoothly. And just as they had been during Peter's original illness, friends, neighbours and customers were absolutely fantastic in the way that they spontaneously rallied round to offer both practical assistance and moral support just when it was most needed. The great kindness and consideration shown by so many people during those often dark and difficult days is something I shall never forget.

Dr Richard Taylor, who had taken over as our GP following Peter Middleton's retirement, was also quite marvellous in the way he looked after us all, regularly popping in on his own initiative to check up on Augusta and Peter, often accompanied by his wife Kay. Kay and Augusta had become great friends and would regularly meet for lunch or coffee, little outings that Augusta looked forward to with enormous pleasure.

She remained fantastically strong psychologically after the sarcoma operation and the course of radio therapy that followed. Physically, however, her recovery turned out to be much more laboured this time. The site of what had been a major operation took a long time to heal properly and was often very painful, making it difficult for her to sit or even lie down for any length of time in comfort. As a result, she started to lose some of her self-confidence, gradually becoming both more fragile and more dispirited. Although she again insisted on going back to work, she had to spend more and more time upstairs resting and less and less time down in the restaurant. And on top of all that she was desperately worried about Peter, far more concerned about him and about me than she was about herself.

Given her weakened state, it was perhaps hardly surprising that in February 2007 the original pancreatic cancer returned. And because she was no longer strong enough, there were limits to how much more chemotherapy she could take.

From then on she went gradually but steadily downhill. She would still make the effort to appear in the restaurant from time to time and in March 2008 we even managed to get out to Portugal together for what was to be the last time, holding what was effectively a farewell supper at the villa for a dozen close friends and members of the family.

Everybody could see what was happening, but Augusta and I never totally gave up hope. We still thought that David Cunningham could fix it, that it was just a matter of holding on until the drugs started working. Even when the cancer spread to her lung and she had to have yet another operation we were still trying to be positive, telling each other: "It's just another operation. It's a bloody nuisance, but it'll be OK."

But, of course, it wasn't. Peter and Helen had already warned Heather, Edward and James that their grandma was gravely ill and that she wasn't going to get better. Heather, who had always been especially close to her 'Nanny', was the worst-affected by this. Edward dealt with it by keeping an emotional distance while James, the youngest and perhaps the most sentimental of the three, was tearful.

Eventually, David Cunningham had to tell me that there was nothing more that he and his team at the Royal Marsden could do for her and on June 30th, 2008 Augusta came home to Priors Hardwick. Over the next days the family and close friends were all able to say their last farewells.

For the final sixteen hours of her life I held her in my arms, lying beside her on our bed at home. Neither then nor at any other time did we ever talk about one of us going without the other. I simply told her over and over again, as I had told her throughout: "We are together now and we will be together for ever."

She finally slipped away on the morning of July 18th, 2008.

Her funeral took place eleven days later at the village church of St Mary's and she was laid to rest in the graveyard there in a spot that was as close as possible to The Butcher's Arms, no more than a hundred yards or so from the front door. Her headstone is clearly visible from our bedroom window.

The little church was packed to overflowing for the service, which was relayed to a marquee on the lawn behind Peter's house across the road where hundreds more people from all over the country had gathered to pay their respects. The total congregation numbered well over one thousand. The fact that so many people from so many different walks of life had come from far and wide to be there was the clearest indication of the enormous affection that Augusta inspired in all those with whom she came into contact, something that was further reflected in the avalanche of cards, letters and emails that cascaded into The Butcher's Arms as the news of her passing spread.

The funeral service was the last to be conducted by the Rev Geoffrey Morris before his retirement as the vicar of St Mary's. He shared the duties with his wife, the Rev Anne Morris, a non-stipendiary minister at All Saints, Leamington, and Monsignor Graham Adams, the catholic priest from the church of The Sacred Heart and Our Lady at Aston-le-Walls. In his opening address, Geoffrey Morris struck exactly the right, uplifting note when he started off by making the point that although it was a desperately sad day it was also a glorious day, a time of mourning but also an opportunity to celebrate the extraordinary life of a very remarkable woman. And these contrasting sentiments were nobly and touchingly reflected in the fine and heartfelt words of tribute spoken during the service by Baroness Knight of Collingtree, David Hobbs and Peter Tahany and also in the poems read out by him, by Sue Moore and by sixteen-year-old granddaughter Heather.

Baroness Knight – formerly Jill Knight MP, and a regular customer and good friend for forty years – praised Augusta as the perfect role model for any wife and mother.

"Everyone whose life has been touched by knowing Augusta will miss her and mourn her," she said. "But how fortunate we were to have known her, for she was a truly inspirational lady."

She went on: "I've never met anyone in all my life who started with as little as Lino and Augusta did, who surmounted so many hurdles, won so many battles, overcame so many difficulties and achieved so much. And although I have the greatest possible admiration and respect for Lino, I really don't think he could have done what he did without Augusta.

"Her love and help have been constant, boundless and limitless, even though sometimes the jobs facing her must have been absolutely daunting. Her contribution to their achievement is truly incalculable. Whether teaching, cooking, working, organising or inventing there is no part of the Pires project that she was not involved in. And on top of all that she was a wonderful mother and grandmother. Our hearts go out to Lino and the family."

Baroness Knight was followed to the lectern by David Hobbs, four generations of whose family have dined regularly at The Butcher's Arms, and he brought smiles as well as tears to the faces of the packed congregation as he recalled fond memories of a close thirty-five year friendship.

Looking back to our arrival in the village, David, who was living just down the road in Upper Boddington at that time, said he could well understand why Augusta had burst into tears when she first set eyes on the pub.

"I used to drop in for the odd pint or two on occasion and it was indeed a very drab, down-at-heel pub," he remembered. "When Lino and Augusta pulled up on a cloudy, rainy day it must have looked dreadful, both inside and out. But Augusta just rolled up her sleeves, moved in and set about improving things where she could.

"Being so local, we were among the first to sample the chicken-in-the-basket that was one of her very early specialities. And while my mother fell under the spell of Lino, we all fell under the spell of Augusta's cooking. As a family, we celebrated thirty-two consecutive Christmas Eves at The Butcher's Arms, a tradition that only ended when I and my wife Margaret finally moved to the USA."

Paying tribute to Augusta, he said: "Everyone who ever came into contact with Augusta loved her – and for a very good reason. She was a loving, caring, compassionate and generous person. But along with her big, soft heart she also had tremendous inner strength and a core of steel." He paused momentarily at that point before sending a ripple of fond laughter through the congregation by adding: "Well, you'd have to have a core of steel to be married to Lino for over fifty years!"

He went on to say: "The fascinating story of Lino and Augusta's journey through life, from modest beginnings in Paiágua to the pinnacle of their achievement here in Priors Hardwick, is a story not only of steely determination, hard work and achievement, but also of love, friendship and a wonderful partnership of soul mates."

Later in the service, Augusta's great friend Sue Moore read the poem 'Lord Of All Pots And Pans', which was written in 1928 by a 19-year-old girl working in domestic service and which seemed simply and touchingly appropriate.

There then followed what was, for me, an especially moving moment when granddaughter Heather bravely got up to read the poem that opens with the line 'Do not stand at my grave and weep'.

Right until the moment that she stood up and walked to the lectern we had not been sure whether she would actually be up to it. The composure that she then showed, in such harrowing circumstances and in front of so many people, was remarkable for a sixteen-year-old. We were so proud of her. I must confess that I had been encouraging her to make the effort, saying that although it would be tough, she would regret it for the rest of her life if she didn't say her piece. And she told me afterwards that I was quite right – that she was so glad that she had managed to do it.

The final reading was by Peter Tahany, whose parents were responsible for bringing Augusta to England in 1960 to be his nanny when he was a new-born baby. Had it not been for the Tahany family, Augusta and I might never have left Portugal, the Butcher's Arms would never have happened and our life story would have been so very different.

Recalling that he had known Augusta for all of his forty-seven years, an emotional Peter told the congregation before reading the poem 'The Little Ship': "In those first two years of my life I was the very fortunate recipient of her unqualified love, her persistently happy disposition and infectious laugh and her unbounded kindness, patience and joy of life - precious gifts I have enjoyed since and which I cherish.

"Augusta shared her natural goodness with me as she did with so many others: a wonderful mother and grandmother, an inspiring wife, a very spoiling chef, an exceedingly warm hostess, a most thoughtful friend and the best nanny ever! I treasure her memory and will always smile when I think of her."

From the depths of grief, I was momentarily buoyed up by the positive emotions of that day. There was something truly wonderful about the way in which everybody present wanted to share only good memories of Augusta. One after another they came up to me to offer condolences, only to end up fondly recalling and recounting their favourite Augusta stories and anecdotes, most of which had to do with her natural warmth, her sense of fun, the loving kindness and generosity that she showed to one and all and the many other endearing qualities that made such a deep and lasting impression on just about everybody she ever came into contact with.

That outpouring of love and affection from so many different people – family, friends, neighbours, staff, customers and business colleagues – helped me to smile through the tears as the funeral developed, just as the Rev Geoffrey Morris had said it should, into a celebration of a life that had been so full of achievement, joy, love and happiness. It had indeed been a glorious send-off.

In the days and weeks and months that have followed I have inevitably found myself struggling to come to terms with my loss. Augusta and I had known each other for almost our entire lives and had lived and worked closely together for well over fifty years, during which time we had rarely been apart. So, her passing left a gaping void in my life that can never really be filled.

Thank goodness for The Butcher's Arms. My busy daily routine there keeps me occupied and focused and to have Peter and Helen working alongside me and living right next door with the grandchildren is a great comfort. Adding to the feel of a genuine family business, Heather and Edward have already started earning extra pocket money by helping out part-time in the restaurant during school holidays and university vacations and James will no doubt soon be doing the same. Apart from that, I am able to enjoy the company of the large extended family represented by our regular customers, so many of whom have become close friends over the years. That has been a wonderful bonus.

However, it is when the last customer has gone home at the end of the evening, when the staff have packed up and left and when the empty restaurant has fallen silent that the loneliness engulfs me. As I close up for the night, turn out the lights and go upstairs to the apartment with only my dog Figo for company – those are the times that I find really difficult.

In the same way, I never go to the villa in Portugal now unless I can find someone else to go with me, either family or friends. I couldn't bear to sit on the terrace on my own, watching those spectacular sunsets over the sea. It would be just too painful.

I have to accept that life will never be quite the same again. But I also have to keep telling myself that I should be thankful for all the fantastic years I shared with Augusta and proud of what we achieved together. It is quite true what everybody says – we were a great team. That was always the secret of The Butcher's Arms' success. And I very much hope that in the years to come, Peter and

Helen will be able to carry on the same great family tradition.

In paying final tribute to Augusta, I can do no better than repeat the words we used in thanking all the many hundreds of people who wrote with messages of sympathy and condolence following her death: "She was a great lady and a woman of substance, kind and gentle, warm and loving and with a wonderful sense of humour; a proud mother and grandmother who lived for her family and who never lost touch with her roots. Memories of Paiágua were enough to reduce her to tears. Many more tears have since been shed for her. Augusta was someone for whom it can truly be said that it was a great privilege to have known her and to have been counted a friend."

To have been loved by such a woman and to have had her by my side throughout so many happy and successful years has been the greatest blessing of my life.

EPILOGUE

It was only recently that I applied for and was granted British citizenship, but I have long regarded England as my true home. And when the time comes, I shall be laid to rest next to Augusta in St Mary's churchyard at Priors Hardwick.

I still have family in Vinha and Paiágua, including my sister-in-law, Maria Dos Santos, and endless cousins; in little country villages like that almost everyone is related in some way. But I have no overwhelming feelings of nostalgia for the place where I was born and grew up. To me, it all seems like a distant part of another life from which, I have to admit, I was only too happy to escape.

Interestingly, apart from the fact that there are now tarmac roads where once there were just rough, stony forest tracks, the overall look of the place hasn't changed that much over the years, except for the fact that, sadly, many of the houses, including the one where I was born, now lie empty and derelict.

There is no future there any more for the younger generations who, just as Augusta and I once did, have long since moved away to seek a better future elsewhere. One or two maintain their old family homes as weekend or holiday retreats or hang on to them out of sentiment, but others, unable to sell because there are simply no buyers, have simply abandoned them and left them to crumble and collapse.

The childhood landmarks, however, all remain, as I pointed out when showing a friend around the area on one of my last visits there with Augusta. Picking my way through the scattered vegetable plots immediately below our old house and then continuing on down the steep hillside to the river below, I could still just about follow the narrow footpath along which I used to walk to school each morning, although now that the road is there it has become very overgrown in parts through lack of use. Moving across the river and into the trees, I could still vividly recall the little frisson of fear I sometimes experienced as I returned home at twilight on winter evenings, startled by sudden sinister sounds from the undergrowth.

Heading on past Silvosa and up over the hill to Paiágua I could recall the exact point at which, emerging from the woods, I would become visible to Augusta as she waited and watched for my arrival from a vantage point in her back yard. And there, on the outskirts of the village, was the little spring where, during the hot summer months, Augusta would be sent by her father to fetch a pitcher of the ice cold, crystal clear drinking water with which he liked to refresh himself after a long hard day in the fields. Further downstream, the rocks in the water still bear the scars of some of my more explosive fishing expeditions.

Strolling through the labyrinth of narrow alleyways in the village itself you can still see the communal bread oven where the village boys would gather to loiter and watch the girls go by – and where they would also lie in wait to ambush me! The steeply sloping village square, where we all used to dance at fiesta time, is exactly the same as it was, with the church on one side and, on the other, the bare concrete platform where the musicians would sit and play.

Also in the square is the house in which the barber-cum-doctor-cum-dentist used to operate, pulling teeth with a pair of pliers – and without any anaesthetic! – in between dispensing traditional herbal remedies and giving people a short-back-and-sides. Close by is the house in which the village tailor used to live and work, making suits for the equivalent of about £2 in today's money. I still get suits, jackets and trousers made-to-measure by his grandson, David Nunes, who now has a very smart shop in the centre of Castelo Branco. He charges a great deal more than £2 these days but is still very good value for money.

At the top end of the square stands the old original schoolhouse. The school itself moved to another building a long time ago and has now closed down altogether. There are no longer any children in the village, except in the summer when families who have kept second homes there come back for weekends and holidays.

Augusta would always get very emotional whenever she returned to Paiágua. I remember an occasion when an elderly aunt found her weeping as she stood outside her old family home, which is now, sadly, showing signs of dilapidation. "You shouldn't be crying," the aunt told her. "Just think how much better your life is now."

But that's the point. It was exactly because she herself was living such a comfortable life that Augusta used to get upset when she thought back to the hardships that her parents had had to endure right up until the end of their days. Looking now at the hovels where we grew up it is difficult to imagine how we managed to put up with such basic, cramped conditions. And yet, because we were young and knew nothing better, it never seemed that much of a problem at the time.

My attitude was always much less sentimental than Augusta's. I shared her aunt's view that we should just be happy that we got away. Augusta would look at the remains of the little one-room extension that I built onto my family's hovel in Vinha as our first home, a space barely big enough to take a modern double bed, and would cry because it seemed so pitiful. I looked upon it with pride as a measure of what I had gone on to achieve in my life.

Augusta's nephew Eric, who worked as a waiter at The Butcher's Arms for many years and who, along with his brother, Joseph, played such an important part in helping me to set up and run the business in the early days before the two of them moved to France to open a restaurant of their own together, eventually retired back to Paiágua, happy to work the fields again while caring for his mother, Augusta's sister, Maria Marques, until her death. I, on the other hand, would never, ever, have dreamed of going back for good, certainly not to Vinha or Paiágua and probably not even to Sintra or Lisbon.

I have occasionally wondered how different things might have been if, for instance, I had managed to persuade my brother-in-law to join me in the café venture in Sintra all those years ago; or if my Godfather had only used the money that I gave him when I left for England to find a little business for me, as I had hoped he might be able to do. I am still convinced that if only I could have got even the smallest start at that time, then with my natural drive, determination and business flair I would have done very well for myself.

Looking back, I do sometimes regret what I see as wasted years, but I have no real complaints about the fact that my destiny turned out to lie a world away in the very different countryside of Warwickshire. In the end, England gave me everything while Portugal gave me nothing.

Home, they say, is where the heart is – and for many years now my heart has been very much in Priors Hardwick. That is where it will remain forever more.

The Royal Marsden Charity Evening Auction
1st February 1998

	Items to be auctioned:	**Price Achieved**
1.	"Links" of London Sterling Silver Desk Clock (*kindly donated by Fred Burrow of Gurit Essex Ltd*)	£550
2.	"The Gates of Althorp, Vision of Heaven" (*an original watercolour kindly donated by Mr and Mrs Elkins of Northampton*)	£500
3.	A collection of McLaren Mercedes Formula 1 Memorabilia. To include a jumper, T-shirt, Polo shirt, baseball cap and computer mouse mat (*kindly donated by Computervision Ltd*)	£125
4.	Use of a Mercedes Benz SLK Sports convertible for a weekend	£450
5.	Two Grandstand tickets with full hospitality for the 1998 Formula 1 British Grand Prix at Silverstone (*kindly donated by Mr Barrie Thrussell of the RAC*)	£800
6.	Use of a stunning Jaguar XK8 sports convertible for three months (*kindly donated by Mr Nick Scheele, Chairman of Jaguar Cars Ltd*)	£3,000
7.	An Imperial (8 bottles) Grahams 1985 vintage port (*donated by The Butcher's Arms*)	£1,500 (1st) £1,200 (2nd)
8.	A Berkeley forge garden bench for two (*kindly donated by Vivienne Barlow of Country Gardens*)	£350

Items to be auctioned:	Price Achieved
9. A day's off-road driving instruction for one person at Land Rover's Jungle Track at Solihull (*kindly donated by John Parkinson of the Rover Group*)	£500
10. A case of 12 bottles of Australian wine made by Brown Brothers – 6 Family Reserve Chardonnay and 6 Cabernet Sauvignon (*kindly donated by Mr Ray Sweby of Faulding Pharmaceuticals plc*)	£425
11. A Panasonic in-car CD tuner, fitted (*kindly donated by David and Hazel Blackwell of Clarendon Motor Services Ltd of Leamington Spa*)	£600
12. A tour for two people of Prodrive's World Championship-winning Rally Team in the morning, followed by lunch and a tour of the Benetton Formula 1 factory in the afternoon (*kindly donated by Mr David Richards and Mr David Lapworth of Prodrive Ltd*)	£600
13. A mobile telephone (*kindly donated by Mr John Chalfin of Intercell Ltd*)	£650
14. A pre-theatre dinner at the Tamarind Indian restaurant and a deluxe double room at the Halcyon Hotel, London (*kindly donated by Mr and Mrs E. Saunders*)	£525
15. Two sets of a child's complete kit in Coventry City FC's home colours and a match ball, the shirts and balls autographed by the players (*kindly donated by Mr J. Reason of Coventry*)	£700
16. A track day in a Caterham 7 doing high-speed passenger laps at Donington Park racing circuit for three people, to include refreshments (*kindly donated by Andrew and Stuart Parker of Team Parker Racing*)	£650

Items to be auctioned:	Price Achieved
17. One week's stay for up to six people in a Cornish country cottage one mile from Rock (*kindly donated by Mrs Jenny Hayward*)	£800
18. Set of four four-wheel drive tyres by "General", fitted (*kindly donated by Mr Alan Baldwin of Southam Tyres*)	£350
19. A lovely garden statue (4ft high) (*kindly donated by Mr and Mrs Jakeman of the Southam Garden Centre*)	£100
20. A day driving a Rover MGF at the racing circuit of your choice. (*kindly donated by John Parkinson of the Rover Group*)	£300
21. A trip to The Butcher's Arms restaurant for lunch, collected and delivered in a vintage 8-litre Bentley - the car that brought Peter and Helen from the church to their wedding reception (*kindly donated by Mr Geoff Parker*)	£400
22. Three gift vouchers for the sum of £100 each to be spent in three of the top clothes shops in Leamington Spa (*kindly donated by Lorraine and John from Feminique, Arias and Status*)	£350
23. A beautiful Portuguese crocheted table cloth, measuring 3 × 1.5 metres, hand-made by Augusta	£1,200
24. A Camping Gaz Ranchero 1100 super gas barbecue (*kindly donated by Mr G Davies of H.E. Philips Ltd of Coventry*)	£470
25. A hair appointment at Rackhams Hair Salon, to include manicure and facial (*kindly donated by Fenella*)	£120
26. "The Computer Lab", a book written and illustrated by Bryony Hill (*kindly donated and signed by Jimmy Hill*)	£100

	Items to be auctioned:	Price Achieved
27.	One year's full double membership of the Warwick Health Club (*kindly donated by Mr and Mrs Jones of Warwick*)	£300
28.	A quantity of marble or granite for kitchen and bathroom surfaces to customer's specification (*kindly donated by Mr Don Bannocks of Bannocks Tigre Marble Co Ltd*)	£750
29.	The use of lovely town house in Salcombe, Devon for a long weekend for up to six people (*kindly donated by Mr and Mrs Postins of Balsall Common*)	£500
30.	A tour of the Aston Martin factory at Newport Pagnell, with use of an Aston Martin DB7 for four days, including track driving at Goodwood racing circuit (*kindly donated by Mr Simon Thrussell of Aston Martin Lagonda Ltd*)	£800
31.	A fabulous weekend for two at the Palacio de Seteais hotel, Sintra, Portugal, including flights from TAP Air Portugal and dinner at the best restaurant in the area, the Curral dos Caprinos	£1,050
32.	Another fabulous weekend for two in the company of Lino and Augusta at their house in Portugal, to include transport (if you don't mind Lino's driving!) and Augusta's cooking	1st $10,000 (£6,300) 2nd £7,500
33.	Two weeks in a six-bedroom house overlooking a championship golf course in Florida (*kindly donated by Mr and Mrs Lamb*)	£3,000
34.	28 days use of Jaguar XK8 or Daimler V8 (*kindly donated by Mr Dennis Stickley*)	£800
35.	One week in a lakeside hotel near Chicago, including flights and use of car (*kindly donated by Mr Gregory Hobbs and Mr Richard Sadiq*	£1,500
36.	Vouchers for a year's hairdressing services (*kindly donated by Pat Dixon of Classics hair and beauty salon*)	£450